Obsession with Justice

The Story of the Deuteronomists

William J. Doorly

Paulist Press/New York/Mahwah, N.J.

222.1506
DoO

*also from William J. Doorly
published by Paulist Press*

Prophet of Justice
Prophet of Love
Isaiah of Jerusalem

ACKNOWLEDGMENTS

The Publisher gratefully acknowledges use of the following material: excerpts from *The Tribes of Yahweh* by Norman K. Gottwald, copyright © 1979 Orbis Books, Maryknoll, New York.

The Scripture quotations contained herein are from the New Revised Standard Version of the Bible, copyrighted, 1989 by the Division of Christian Education of the National Council of the Churches of Christ in the United States of America, and are used by permission. All rights reserved.

Library of Congress Cataloging-in-Publication Data

Doorly, William J., 1931–
    Obsession with justice : the story of the Deuteronomists / by William J. Doorly.
        p.   cm.
    Includes bibliographical references and index.
    ISBN 0-8091-3487-X (paper)
    1. Deuteronomistic history (Biblical criticism)   2. Justice—Biblical teaching.   3. Levites.   4. Jews—History—To 586 B.C.—Historiography.   I. Title.
    BS1286.5.D66   1994
    222'.06—dc20   94-15328
                                                        CIP

Published by Paulist Press
997 Macarthur Boulevard
Mahwah, NJ 07430

Printed and bound in the
United States of America

TABLE OF CONTENTS

GUIDE TO CHARTS AND MAPS

ACKNOWLEDGMENTS

It is my good fortune to have as an editor, Father Lawrence Boadt, Old Testament editor of the Paulist Press. Father Boadt not only carefully read and inspected the manuscript for this book but took the time to provide me with a substantial list of suggestions and recommendations. Each item on the list was helpful to me in raising questions and providing insight, enabling me to increase the clarity of the manuscript. I am indebted to him and grateful for his support and careful attention, not only with this book, but with previous books of mine published by the Paulist Press.

I would also like to acknowledge the logistical support provided by the Main Line Corporation of Jupiter/Tequesta, Florida. Main Line provided the computer hardware and software for the production of the manuscript, much of which was done in Vero Beach, Florida. I am especially grateful to Noe Santamarina, President, and also John Santamarina.

This book is for
Mark Edward and Louise Renee
from their father, with love.

INTRODUCTION

This book is an attempt to present an account of a zealous, Levitical priesthood, which in the late 7th century was responsible for the emergence of the first version of the Hebrew Bible. During the reign of King Josiah (640–609 B.C.E.), only decades before the end of Judah as an independent political entity, something entirely new came into existence in the religious life of the indigenous people of the small nation of Judah in southeastern Palestine. For the first time, Yahweh, their ancient God of six centuries, spoke to his people through *writings on a scroll*. Previously Yahweh had spoken to their ancestors in other ways, including dreams, visions, with a voice of his own, through divine messengers (angels), through the human voice of chosen messengers (prophets), and through natural phenomena.

Holy scripture first emerged when the book of the law was discovered in the temple of Jerusalem in 621 B.C.E. during an official effort to clean and repair the temple. Shortly thereafter a monumental history of Israel appeared which started with Joshua and ended with Josiah.

The collection of laws discovered in the temple was the torah which appears as the core of the book of Deuteronomy (chapters 12 through 26) in our English Bible. This torah, with additional material surrounding it, was placed before the "history" of Israel which this zealous priestly circle produced, and served as an introduction.

Many, many centuries later, Biblical scholars would call this history the Deuteronomistic history (DH),[1] and the zealous priesthood which produced it, the Deuteronomists. This priesthood never called itself by this name, and the word Deuteronomist does not appear in the Bible. They were Levitical priests and scribes with their roots firmly established in the traditions of the northern king-

1

dom of Israel. During the reign of King Josiah they contrasted themselves and their theology with an equally zealous, but competing
priesthood which promoted an entirely different theology. The competing priesthood has been identified with the name Aaronids.

The *Deuteronomists*, these late 7th century Jerusalem Levites,
in addition to producing the first version of the book of Deuteronomy
and the earliest version of their tremendously influential history of
Israel, DH (Joshua, Judges, Samuel, Kings), also produced updated
versions of four 8th century prophets, whose oracles they had preserved and studied. These 8th century prophets were Amos of Tekoa,
Hosea ben Beeri, Micah of Moresheth, and Isaiah of Jerusalem.

One of the goals of this small circle of Levites was to centralize
and standardize the religion of Yahweh in Jerusalem, under their
leadership, with their particular theology as the foundation. Under
no circumstances could they have imagined the tremendous influence they were to have on the history of religion and culture of
western civilization for the next several thousand years. In this book
we will discover that this circle, which modestly claimed to be preservers and defenders of Israel's ancient past, was in fact an innova-
tive and creative force which gave birth to ideas and perceptions in
the area of religion which were equal to, or greater than, the contribution made by the philosophers and mathematicians of ancient
Greece.

Their seventh century B.C.E. activities provided the turning
point for ancient Israel. There is a possibility that without their
contribution you and I would know as much about ancient Israel as
we know about Edom, Moab, or Bashan.

Terms Defined

Before we turn to chapter 1, where we will locate the activity of
the Deuteronomists in the chronology of Israel, there are logistical
matters to deal with.

(1) During the last three decades there has been progress in our
scholarly understanding of the Deuteronomistic history. Progress
means change, and change produces new vocabulary. As the student
reads the many fine books written about the subject at hand, he or
she may be confused by the alternation of the terms *Deuteronomistic*
and *Deuteronomic*. In this book we will try to follow the practice of
an important book on the subject written by Richard Elliot Fried-

CHART 1
CHRONOLOGY OF ISRAEL/JUDAH B.C.E.

1220	Emergence of Israel in the highlands of Canaan, a hilly and mountainous strip running parallel to the Jordan Valley, from Galilee in the north to the Negev in the south.
1020	Emergence of the monarchy with Saul as king.
1000	David emerges as king, first recognized only in Judah. The northern tribes eventually came to Hebron and asked David to become king of a united kingdom. Jerusalem becomes the new capital city.
970	Solomon begins reign.
930	Rehoboam, son of Solomon, becomes king of Judah. The northern area makes Jeroboam king of Israel.
750–700	Social prophets make their appearance delivering oracles critical of the decision makers in Samaria and Jerusalem. Four of these social critics whose oracles have been preserved are Hosea, Amos, Isaiah, and Micah.
722	Samaria is captured by the Assyrians, and Israel (the northern kingdom) comes to an end. Some citizens are taken into captivity, some remain in Israel, others migrate to Judah. Israel had lasted for 208 years.
621	The book of the law (proto-Deuteronomy) is discovered in the temple while repairs are under way during the reign of Josiah (640–609).
609	Josiah is killed in battle with an Egyptian army led by Pharaoh Neco at Meggido.
597	Jerusalem is captured by the Babylonians (Chaldeans). Many are carried into captivity.
587/6	The walls of Jerusalem and the temple are destroyed by the Babylonians. Judah ends as an independent political entity. Judah lasted for 343 years after the death of Solomon. That was 135 years longer than Israel, the northern kingdom.
539	Cyrus the Persian captures Babylon and proclaims that captured people may return to their homeland. The first group of Judahites return to Jerusalem.

man, *The Exile and Biblical Narrative.*[2] *Deuteronomic* will be used to refer to the torah, the direct influence of the torah, chapters 12–26 (or early parts of the torah), and to early portions of Deuteronomy. *Deuteronomistic* will refer to the entire Deuteronomistic history.[3]

One of the contributing reasons for the confusion in the use of the two terms (Deuteronomic and Deuteronomistic) is the result of a common practice of scholars to refer to the influence of the book of Deuteronomy on the history, DH, which follows Deuteronomy in the Bible (Joshua through Kings). The student may get the impression that the book of Deuteronomy was complete before the emergence of DH. This was not the case. Deuteronomy as a book grew in many stages, and was enlarged along with DH, *rather than prior to DH.* What this means is that there are Deuteronomistic portions of the book of Deuteronomy. In chapter 10 we will discuss this concept and explain the growth of Deuteronomy in five stages.

While it is necessary to be aware of the problem of distinguishing between the terms *Deuteronomic* and *Deuteronomistic*, it can be a subtle distinction, and I believe that the reader should not be overly concerned if the two terms become confused.

Of more concern are items 2 and 3 below.

(2) In this book we will frequently use the term DH for Deuteronomistic history.

(3) We will frequently refer to "the Deuteronomist," in the singular, even though the activity referred to may involve the effort of two or more members of the circle.

NOTES

1.   Martin Noth first called DH the Deuteronomistic history in 1943. He did not distinguish between the Josianic history and the exilic redaction. He believed that the author was exilic.

2.   Richard Elliott Friedman, *The Exile and Biblical Narrative*, Harvard Semitic Monographs (Chico: Scholars Press, 1981).

3.   The closer the activity discussed by an author to the discovery of the torah, the more likely he or she is to use the word Deuteronomic (or deuteronomic, without the first letter capitalized). For example, in an introduction to a commentary on Deuteronomy we read the following:

The activities of the deuteronomic school in the seventh century BC, resulting in Deuteronomy and later in the *deuteronomistic* historical work, are not far separated from this time.

The interesting word here is *later*. It seems to imply a break in time between Deuteronomic activity and Deuteronomistic activity. The reader may get the impression that a change of personnel has taken place, with a later group or circle being influenced by an earlier circle. While there may be some truth in this, it will be our premise that members of the Deuteronomic circle were also the Deuteronomists who produced the Josianic edition of the Deuteronomistic history (DH), and it is even possible that some of the persons who produced the Josianic history may also have participated in the Exilic edition of the Deuteronomistic history.

Part I

Chapter 1

THE FIRST EDITION
OF THE HEBREW BIBLE

In order to understand the Bible it is necessary to know when and how it came into existence. It is the premise of this book that *holy scriptures* (writings recognized and accepted as a revelation from Yahweh) did not play a significant role in ancient Israel until several decades before the final destruction of Judah as a political entity (See chart #1, Chronology).

The date assigned to the final destruction of the temple and the walls of Jerusalem by the Chaldeans, whom we know as Babylonians, is 586 B.C.E. Ten years earlier (597), Nebuchadnezzar, the king of Babylon, had carried away a large portion of the population of Jerusalem into Babylonian captivity, but the walls of Jerusalem, along with the temple of Yahweh in Jerusalem, had remained standing.

Ten years passed before the Babylonians decided that the officials remaining in Judah could no longer be trusted to support Babylonian interests in the area of Jerusalem. So in 586 the city and the temple were destroyed and a second group of Judahites were carried away into captivity.

> In . . . the nineteenth year of King Nebuchadnezzar, king of Babylon—Nebuzaradan, the captain of the bodyguard, a servant of the king of Babylon, came to Jerusalem. And he burned the house of the LORD, and the king's house and all the houses of Jerusalem; every great house he burned down. And all the army of the Chaldeans . . . broke down the walls around Jerusalem (2 Kings 25:8–10).

9

At that time some Judahites were left behind in the region with Gedaliah appointed as governor by the king of Babylon (Jeremiah 40:11). Because Jerusalem lay in ruins, Gedaliah attempted to govern from Mizpah, a small town near Jerusalem. With him was one of the greatest Israelites who ever lived:

> Then Jeremiah went to Gedaliah the son of Ahikam, at Mizpah, and dwelt with him among the people who were left in the land (Jeremiah 40:6).

Shortly thereafter Gedaliah was assassinated and Jeremiah and Baruch his scribe were carried away to Egypt against their will by a group of fearful Judahites.

Reviewing the tragic events associated with the fall of Jerusalem, and the two-stage carrying away of Jerusalem's population into foreign captivity, it is easy to forget that only 40 years before these events, Jerusalem had experienced a significant period of security, prosperity, and optimism during the reign of Josiah (640–609). At the time of Josiah, Assyria, Judah's ancient military and political enemy from the east for almost 300 years, was in a period of decline from which she would not recover. For Judah and Jerusalem the final decline of Assyria looked like the dawn of a golden age. The temple was in the process of major restoration, financed in part by collections from the citizens of Jerusalem, and gifts from visitors and interested persons from the rural areas of Judah. With Assyrian power distracted and crumbling, Judah, under Josiah's leadership, would have an opportunity to regain northern territories which had once belonged to the united kingdom of David's Israel.

During the reign of Josiah however, something infinitely more significant than the repair of the temple and the rebuilding of Judah's political stability was taking place. This activity, which can be viewed in retrospect as revolutionary, was taking place within a small circle of zealous Levitical priests located in Jerusalem, which included among its circle some scribes and prophets.

Within this circle it was understood for the first time that Yahweh, the ancient God of Israel, was about to reveal his person and his will to his people in a new medium, the written word. The production of scrolls was a major activity of this circle, along with promotion and support of a massive reformation of the religious practices of Judah and Jerusalem. This small circle eventually became known to scholars as *The Deuteronomists*. The members of this circle, like the citizens of Judah, could not have guessed that the clock was running out for Judah as an independent political entity, and that the small nation was close to extinction. The scrolls which this circle produced would become the heart of what future generations would call the Hebrew Bible, and Christians would call the Old Testament. The scrolls which this circle produced included the following:

(1) An introduction, consisting of the book of the law, *sepher hatorah*, with additional words attributed to Moses, was the first scroll of the collection. As we will see, putting a speech into the mouth of an ancient hero, always a champion of Yahweh, was a common literary practice of ancient Israel. This introduction to DH became known as the book of Deuteronomy.

(2) A lengthy history of Israel followed, using many sources, beginning with Joshua and culminating with Josiah.[1] Among other things, this history (first called the Deuteronomistic history by Martin Noth), described accurately by many scholars as a theological history, explained why Yahweh had allowed the destruction of the northern kingdom of Israel by Assyria. It also explained why and how the southern kingdom of Judah would survive with Yahweh's blessing.

(3) Following the theological history was a new edition of four 8th century prophets, Hosea, Amos, Micah, and Isaiah of Jerusalem. Scholars refer to these editions as the Josianic editions of these prophets. (These four prophetic books are not identical to the books as they now appear in our Bible because all four books would be further expanded, during, and in some cases after, the exilic period.)[2]

An Age of Scrolls

The period of Josiah's reign coincided with an interest in the production of scrolls throughout the entire area of the ancient Near East. Asshurbanipal, the king of Assyria, died in 627, six years before the discovery of the book of the law in the temple. Asshurbanipal is best known for his massive collection of writings in a library at Nineveh. At the same time in Egypt, under Psammetichus I, there was a noted increase in scroll production tied to a renewal of interest in ancient Egyptian cultic practices.[3]

Since we are suggesting that during the reign of Josiah the Deuteronomists perceived for the first time that Yahweh was about to reveal his will to his people through the written word, we should clarify this issue. Numerous writings, belonging to both the monarchy and to several priesthoods, no doubt pre-dated the reign of Josiah. A notable example would be the document which scholars have called the "J" (Jahweh, or Yahweh) history of the ancient world.[4] This J document is generally believed to have appeared during the reign of David or Solomon. Sometime following the division of the nation after the death of Solomon a revision of the J document appeared in the north. The expansions to J have been referred to as the "E" (Elohim) document. These writings (J and E) obviously predated the scrolls produced by the Deuteronomists during the reign of Josiah. In addition to these there were other scrolls, such as the succession narrative, the story of the last years of David, one of the many sources which the Deuteronomists used in compiling their history (See our chapter 5). While we must acknowledge the existence of scrolls which later were incorporated in the growing body of writings recognized as scripture, we are suggesting that during the reign of Josiah a new age of revelation, involving writing, began. The report of Josiah's response to the reading of the book of the law has no precedent in our knowledge of ancient Judah.

> And when the king heard the words of the book of the law, he rent his clothes. . . . "Go, inquire of the LORD for me, and for the people, and for all Judah, concerning the words of this book that has been found; for great is the wrath of the LORD that is kindled against us, because our fathers have not obeyed the words of this book, to do all according to what is written concerning us" (2 Kings 22:11–13).

During the Babylonian captivity, which followed the destruction of Jerusalem, Yahweh's people would became people of the book. But it was during the reign of Josiah (640–609) that the Deuteronomists put together the first edition of *the book,* around which the lives of the exilic community would revolve.

Who were the Deuteronomists? What did the first edition of the Bible contain? What happened to the Deuteronomists? This is the story which we will attempt to tell in this study.

NOTES

1.   Scholars have recently concluded that the first edition of the Deuteronomistic history ended with Josiah. We will explain the obvious reasons for this conclusion in our chapter 4, entitled JOSH-

UA AND JOSIAH. The student can consult the following works: Frank Moore Cross, *Canaanite Myth and Hebrew Epic* (Cambridge: Harvard University Press, 1973). Richard Elliot Friedman, *The Exile and Biblical Narrative*, Harvard Semitic Monographs (Chico: Scholars Press, 1981). R. D. Nelson, *The Double Redaction of the Deuteronomistic History* (Sheffield: JSOT Press, 1981). Andrew D. H. Mayes, *The Story of Israel between Settlement and Exile* (London: SCM Press, 1983).

2. We are suggesting that the first edition of the Hebrew Bible consisted of Deuteronomy, the first edition of DH (Joshua, Judges, Samuel, Kings), and four updated collections of these 8th century prophets: Hosea, Amos, Isaiah, Micah.

3. A. D. H. Mayes in *Deuteronomy* (Grand Rapids: Eerdmans, 1979), 83, writes, "Herrmann in *Probleme*, 169f . . . refers to this time as a renaissance, not just the reviving of old norms and ideas, but the proclamation of new norms and ideas through the editing of traditions."

4. A recent complete study of the "J" history is found in the book by Robert B. Coote and David Robert Ord, *The Bible's First History* (Philadelphia: Fortress Press, 1989).

Chapter 2

THEOLOGY, HISTORY, AND FOLKLORE

In ancient Israel separation of church and state was not considered a virtue. Religion and politics went hand in hand. They were closer than two sides of the same coin. It is not surprising therefore that our story of the Deuteronomists begins with a significant political and economic event, the end of the united kingdom, and its split into two nations following the death of Solomon in 930 B.C.E.

The first Bible history of Israel (the history produced by the Deuteronomists) records events which indicate that there were always tensions between the north and the south, Israel and Judah. Scholars have noted the uniqueness of the tribe of Judah. When Israel first emerged in the highlands of Canaan as a nation of subsistence farmers late in the 13th century, it is possible that Judah was already an alliance of tribes consisting of Judeans, Calebites, Kenites, and others.

Late in the 11th century, following the death of Saul (a Benjaminite), the tribe of Judah refused to recognize Saul's son Ishbosheth as monarch. And the tribes of the north refused to recognize David (a Judean) as king. David reigned in Hebron for seven years as king of Judah before he was accepted by the north as king of all Israel. Eventually David emerged as the best choice for the nation. After seven years

> . . . all the elders of Israel came to the king at Hebron; and King David made a covenant with them at Hebron before the LORD, and they anointed David king over Israel (2 Samuel 5:3).

The united kingdom continued to endure less than a century, from 1020 until Solomon's death in 930, a period of 90 years. On

14

Solomon's death, his son, Rehoboam, became king in his place. Unfortunately for the line of David, the masses of Israel were not willing to accept Rehoboam as king.

The Deuteronomistic History

It is interesting to keep in mind that our source for information concerning the Deuteronomists is the history which the circle produced. It consists of the books of Joshua, Judges, Samuel, and Kings. As the name indicates, Deuteronomistic history, this history was produced by the circle of scribes, priests, and prophets whose identity and character we are trying to uncover. It would be helpful to have other independent detailed historical sources to supply the kind of information which the Deuteronomistic history presents. The closest thing that we do have, of course, is a much later Bible history found in the books of Chronicles. However the production of this second history was dependent on the first, the Deuteronomistic history (DH), and was influenced by it in many unavoidable ways. Comparing the many ways in which DH influenced the books of Chronicles is a study in itself, and it is not our purpose in this book to deal with this subject.[1]

The truth is that we are almost entirely dependent on DH (the Deuteronomistic history) for all of our information about Israel from the settlement in the land (mid 13th century) to the fall of Judah (586). Archaeology has provided us with some valuable inscriptions from Egypt, Assyria, and Babylon.

To begin our understanding of DH we can look at three different types of material produced by the author, or authors, in relating the events which we have made reference to as our starting point, the political separation of the 10 northern tribes from the tribe of Judah following the death of Solomon.

The three types of material are:

1. theology,
2. historical narrative, and,
3. story, or folklore.

Theology

In the scripture passage which follows, the author of DH informs the reader of the theological reasons why the northern tribes

were taken away from Solomon's son. Read this passage carefully
and you will discover important key elements of the theology of the
Deuteronomists.

> For when Solomon was old his wives turned away his heart
> after other gods; and his heart was not wholly true to the
> LORD his God, as was the heart of David his father. For
> Solomon followed Astarte the goddess of the Sidonians, and
> after Milcom the abomination of the Ammonites. So Solo-
> mon did what was evil in the sight of the LORD, and did not
> wholly follow the LORD, as David his father had done. . . .
> And the LORD was angry with Solomon because his heart
> had turned away from the LORD. . . . Therefore the LORD
> said to Solomon, "Since this has been your mind and you
> have not kept my covenant and my statutes which I com-
> manded you, I will surely tear the kingdom from you and
> give it to your servant. . . . But I will give one tribe to your
> son, for the sake of David my servant and for the sake of
> Jerusalem which I have chosen" (1 Kings 11:4–13).

The above passage is a theological explanation of why the house
of David lost the ten northern tribes following Solomon's death. The
passage is drenched in Deuteronomistic theology. We will identify
four examples.

(1) The first is the use of the word heart (Hebrew, *lebab*). in 1
Kings 11:4 (twice) and verse 9:

> And the LORD was angry with Solomon, because his *heart*
> had turned away from the LORD.

The word heart is a key word in Deuteronomy. If you started
reading the Bible from the beginning, Genesis 1:1, and if you had a
mind as specialized as a digital computer (be thankful you don't) you
would notice the following. The Hebrew word *lebab* (heart) appears
in the book of Deuteronomy 41 times. In Exodus it appears a few
times in reference to personal religion, in Leviticus once, and in
Numbers once.

When the systematic Bible reader gets to the book of Deuteronomy there is a new mood, a new tone, a new theology. Although the
book of Deuteronomy has been recognized as the fifth book of the
pentateuch for 2000 years, it does not share the essential character
of the first four books (the tetrateuch). The first four books are made

up of at least three primary sources. The character of the first four books (tetrateuch) was determined to a large extent by the third of the three sources, the priestly source (P) which was the latest source. An exilic and post-exilic priestly circle (P) had the most influence in combining and placing the words, sentences, and paragraphs (this editorial process is called redaction) of the tetrateuchal books in their final, canonical form.

Deuteronomy however is chiefly the work of *one* school. This school, or circle, did not have the same theology or philosophy of history as the priestly circle (P), and therefore the student/reader feels the changes in environment as he or she begins reading Deuteronomy. Not only is there a new mood, a new tone, and a new theology, there also is a new vocabulary.

The use of the word heart is but one example of the new vocabulary the reader encounters.

Another thing that a computer-like mind would notice in Deuteronomy, or an analytical reader for that matter, is that the Deuteronomy law code, chapters 12 through 26, is the only collection of law which contains laws referring to kings. And one of them certainly has Solomon in mind:[2]

> And he (the king) shall not multiply wives for himself, lest his *heart* turn away (Deuteronomy 17:17).

Noting the repeated, constant use of the word *heart* in Deuteronomy is very important to our understanding of the uniqueness of the book. The word *heart* takes us below the level of action and behavior to the level of motivation. In Deuteronomy the reader meets a new, deeper understanding of religious behavior, the behavior of humans toward God. In the first four books of the Bible there is nothing which explicitly comes close to this awareness of motivation behind the behavior of God's people. It is no accident then that the most popular words in the book of Deuteronomy are:

> . . . and you shall love the LORD your God with all your *heart*, and with all your soul, and with all your might (Deuteronomy 6:5).

And immediately following are these words:

> And these words which I command you this day shall be upon your *heart* (Deuteronomy 6:6).

(2) There are four themes or concerns which characterize the school of the Deuteronomists of the late 7th century (during the reign of Josiah) which appear in the theological explanation of why Yahweh took the ten northern tribes from the house of David. The first, as we have mentioned above is indicated by the author's concern for the *heart*, or the motivational level of Solomon's behavior. The second theme is the need for cultic purity. The author tells us Solomon did not value it:

> For Solomon followed Astarte the goddess of the Sidonians, and after Milcom the abomination of the Ammonites. . . . Then Solomon built a high place for Chemosh the abomination of Moab, and for Molech the abomination of the Ammonites, on the mountain east of Jerusalem. And so he did for all his foreign wives, who burned incense and sacrificed to their gods (1 Kings 11:5–8).

Cultic purity for the Deuteronomist refers to the practice of restricting religious behavior to the worship of Yahweh, and eliminating, what the Deuteronomist identified as Assyrian and/or Canaanite practice. Participation in the worship of other gods is forbidden. The collection of law in Deuteronomy begins with these words:

> These are the statutes and ordinances which you shall be careful to do in the land which the LORD, the God of your fathers, has given you to possess, all the days that you live upon the earth. You shall surely destroy all the places where the nations which you shall dispossess served their gods, upon the high mountains and upon the hills and under every green tree; you shall tear down their altars, and dash in pieces their pillars and burn their Asherim with fire; you shall hew down the graven images of their gods, and destroy their name out of that place (Deuteronomy 12:1–3).

The first two characteristics of the Deuteronomistic theology which we have noted by reading the passage critical of Solomon are (1) the role of the *heart,* or motivational level in true religion (Solomon's wives turned away his heart from the LORD), and (2) the need for cultic purity, disallowing the worship of other gods, and practices pleasing to them.

(3) The third element is the need to keep the law.

> Therefore the LORD said to Solomon . . . you have not kept
> my covenant and my statutes which I have commanded
> you. I will surely tear the kingdom from you and give it to
> your servant [Jeroboam] (1 Kings 11:11).

The Deuteronomic concept of keeping the covenant, of which we will
have more to say later, implies the observation of the *conditions* of
the covenant. The conditions were the laws and statutes recorded in
the Deuteronomic torah, Deuteronomy chapters 12–26.

(4) The fourth theological element to note is the mention of
Yahweh's choosing of Jerusalem. In spite of Solomon's sins, Yahweh
would allow the house of David to keep the territory of Judah:

> . . . for the sake of Jerusalem which I have chosen (1 Kings
> 11:13).

These are the four elements of Deuteronomic theology portrayed in
the theological explanation of why the house of David lost the ten
northern tribes: (1) Solomon's heart was not right with Yahweh, (2)
Solomon encouraged the worship of other gods besides Yahweh
[Astarte, Milcom, Molech, Chemosh], (3) Solomon did not keep the
law which provided the conditions of the covenant, however, (4) his
son would keep the territory of Judah for the sake of Jerusalem
because Jerusalem was chosen by Yahweh. In Deuteronomy we are
told that Yahweh would choose a place to make his name dwell there
(Deuteronomy 12:11).

Historical Narrative

In our inspection of what passed in those days for "historical
fact" we turn to 1 Kings, chapter 12.

> Rehoboam went to Shechem, for all Israel had come to She-
> chem to make him king . . . and all the assembly of Israel
> came and said to Rehoboam, "Your father made our yoke
> heavy. Now therefore lighten the hard service of your father
> and his heavy yoke upon us, and we will serve you." He said
> to them, "Depart for three days then come again to me." So
> the people went away. . . .
> So Jeroboam and all the people came to Rehoboam the
> third day as the king said. . . . And the king answered the

people harshly, and forsaking the counsel which the old men had given him, and spoke to them according to the counsel of the young men, saying "My father made your yoke heavy but I will add to your yoke" (1 Kings 12: 1–5, 12–14).

In ancient times there was no such thing as *objective* historical fact. The resources for historical research did not exist in ancient Palestine, and concepts of *history* as you and I think of history were thousands of years in the future of western civilization. As a matter of fact there are many today who would argue that *all* history is subjective, even modern history. When an event takes place in society, there are too many contributing factors and influences and too many actors involved to later determine "without a doubt" exactly what happened, and who did what for what reason. The most obvious example is the reporting of the assassination of President John Fitzgerald Kennedy. There were hundreds of eyewitnesses, a filmed account, and a commission appointed by President Lyndon B. Johnson. The commission produced 16 volumes of text on its investigation. Several decades later it is impossible to find two people who agree on exactly what happened, who was involved, and what were the motives.

Now imagine, if you will, someone in ancient Israel explaining a decisive, important event in his nation's history, a complicated meeting which took place almost *300 years* before the author was born.

We are now looking at a passage of scripture (2 Kings, chapter 12) which purports to tell what happened when the son of Solomon was rejected as king by the ten northern tribes. Why call it *historical* narrative? There are good reasons to use this term. As you read this passage you know you are not reading an overtly theological account such as the account of Solomon's heart being turned away from Yahweh. This passage (2 Kings 12) deals with secular events on an historical level. Here we are dealing with the traditional stuff of history, economics and politics. That doesn't mean that there are not theological implications in this political account. There are theological elements in all historical discussions, and there are historical elements in most theological discussions. When we call the passage about Rehoboam and the elders of the ten tribes historical, we are identifying its characteristic tone and feeling. The entire affair at Shechem is handled on such a mundane level that either the author or an editor thought it was necessary to remind the reader that Yahweh was playing a role. For this reason the following *editorial comment* was inserted into the account:

Wherefore the king hearkened not to the people, for the cause was from Yahweh, that he might perform his saying, which Yahweh had spoken to Ahijah the Shilonite unto Jeroboam the son of Nebat (1 Kings 12:15).

When this narrative of Rehoboam at Shechem was written into DH it was an ancient tradition, and since the Deuteronomists came from the north (and for other reasons) it is safe to say that the viewpoint of this narrative was produced with a northern bias.

What does the narrative tell us? It tells us that the social and economic burdens which Solomon placed on the masses of Israel, burdens of taxation and mandatory participation in building projects (forced labor),[3] caused the masses of the people to rebel and seek relief from the oppressive practices by appealing to Solomon's son, Rehoboam, for a change of practices found intolerable. The Deuteronomists placed emphasis on the egalitarian values of pre-monarchical Israel. In this account the old men with Rehoboam, Solomon's son, look to the practices and values of a past time, but the young advisors look to protect their privileged position dependent on an oppressive monarchy. Rehoboam took the advice of the young advisors:

And the king answered the people harshly, and forsaking the counsel which the old men had given him, he spoke to them according to the counsel of the young men, saying, "My father made your yoke heavy, but I will add to your yoke; my father chastised you with whips, but I will chastise you with scorpions" (1 Kings 12:14–15).

This account of the secession of the northern tribes, leaving the house of David with only the tribe of Judah (and perhaps Benjamin, v. 21), has several problems. For one thing the causes given for the action are social and economic. In the theological narrative (1 Kings 11:1–13), the cause given is the turning of Solomon's heart by his foreign wives. Also interesting is the question raised by the selection of Shechem, a northern shrine, as the site for negotiations between Rehoboam and the people of Israel.

Rehoboam went to Shechem, for all Israel had come to Shechem to make him king (1 Kings 12:1).

Jerusalem would have been the logical place for the coronation of Rehoboam. We will answer this question in chapter 13, "Going Back to the Beginning."

The historian ends the account with a typically Deuteronomistic comment, characteristic of the entire history, the prophecy-fulfillment pattern.[4]

So the king did not listen to the people, because it was a turn of affairs brought about by the LORD that he might fulfill his word, which the LORD had spoken by Ahijah the Shilonite to Jeroboam son of Nebat (1 Kings 12:15).

And this brings us to a third form of literature found in DH, folklore.

Folklore

Jeroboam is a name which appears frequently in the Deuteronomistic history. Every king of Israel will be accused of walking in the sins of Jeroboam. We will discuss his *sins* in our chapter 3, "The Sins of Jeroboam and the Shrine at Bethel."

There are many incidents included in DH which cannot be called history. Although they do not have the feeling of history they are related to the theological explanations such as the example cited above concerning the turning of Solomon's heart. They are stories, often about prophets and significant persons such as kings, and they reveal something about the culture from which they emerged. The Deuteronomists made a decision to include these stories in their history, and in so doing distinguished their work from the sources which they used such as the royal chronicles.[5] We read of the meeting between Ahijah and Jeroboam on the open road:

. . . Ahijah laid hold of the new garment he was wearing and tore it into twelve pieces. He then said to Jeroboam: Take for yourself ten pieces; for thus says the LORD the God of Israel, "See I am about to tear the kingdom from the hand of Solomon, and give you ten tribes" (1 Kings 11:30–31).

The inclusion of this story indicates several significant Deuteronomistic characteristics in addition to the prophecy-fulfillment pattern. For example Ahijah is called a *nabi*, which is the Deutero-

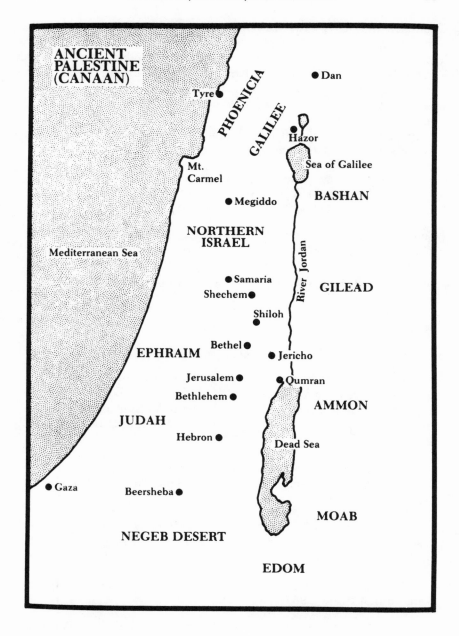

ANCIENT
PALESTINE
(CANAAN)

● Dan

Tyre ●

PHOENICIA

GALILEE

Hazor ●

Sea of Galilee

Mt.
Carmel

BASHAN

● Megiddo

NORTHERN
ISRAEL

Mediterranean Sea

River Jordan

● Samaria

Shechem ●

GILEAD

Shiloh ●

Bethel ●

EPHRAIM

● Jericho

Jerusalem ●

● Qumran

Bethlehem ●

AMMON

JUDAH

Hebron ●

Dead Sea

● Gaza

Beersheba ●

MOAB

NEGEB DESERT

EDOM

nomist's favorite Hebrew word for a prophet. Also, the element in the account which makes it a story, that is the tearing of the garment into 12 pieces, with ten being given to Jeroboam, reminds us that DH was composed to be read at public gatherings for the purpose of education and indoctrination. Persons in the congregation, the hearers, would be likely to remember this incident and repeat it for their families and neighbors.

But the most significant element of the story is that it is a written account of the word of Yahweh as delivered by a prophet.

> . . . for thus says the LORD the God of Israel, "See I am about to tear the kingdom from the hand of Solomon, and give you ten tribes" (1 Kings 11:30–31).

The Deuteronomists, with their reverence for the prophets as ones who spoke words for Yahweh, not only produced the first scrolls to be accepted as containing the words of the LORD, but produced, in the days of Josiah, scrolls which would be recognized in their entirety as holy scriptures.

NOTES

1.   There are historical discrepancies between Chronicles and DH. We will refer to a few of these throughout this book. A definitive book on this subject is available, by Steven L. McKenzie, *The Chronicler's Use of the Deuteronomistic History* (Atlanta: Scholars Press, 1984).

2.   Some scholars believe that this law was originally written for Omri, an important northern king. That does not exclude its later adaptation for Solomon, however.

3.   1 Kings 11:27–28 mentions the forced labor of the house of Joseph which Solomon used to build Millo and close a gap in the city wall.

4.   See *Reading the Old Testament*, by Lawrence Boadt (Mahwah: Paulist Press, 1984), page 379.

5.   We will list the external sources used by the Deuteronomists in compiling their history in chapter 5. Also see our chart, Primary Sources.

Chapter 3

THE SINS OF JEROBOAM AND THE
SHRINE AT BETHEL

Where did the Deuteronomists come from? Almost all scholars believe that they came from the northern kingdom of Israel. They were Levitical priests who fled to Judah and Jerusalem at the time that Assyrian armies destroyed Samaria (722) putting an end to Israel, the northern kingdom, as a political entity.

Whereas some scholars believe that they came from the area of Shechem, between Mount Ebal and Mount Gerizim, others believe that they came from the shrine at Shiloh. Since the two locations were only ten miles apart,[1] it is possible that two Levitical priesthoods were related, or that one priesthood served at both shrines. There is one scripture reference which associates the two locations.

> . . . eighty men arrived from Shechem and Shiloh (Jeremiah 41:4).

It is not crucial to decide between Shechem and Shiloh as the exact location which the circle known as the Deuteronomists considered its ancient home. There may have been two ancient Levitical priesthoods which merged after the destruction of Israel (722) when they arrived in Judah and found it expedient to share their common heritage from the north. It is important however to be familiar with the role played by both northern shrines, Shechem and Shiloh, in the Deuteronomic and Deuteronomistic scriptures.

Shechem

There are three important references to Shechem.

(1) In Deuteronomy, after the presentation of the torah (chapters 12 to 26) Moses commands the people to build an altar on Mount Ebal of unhewn stones and "offer burnt offerings on it to the LORD your God" (Deuteronomy 27:4–7). Then Moses divided the tribes into two groups with six assigned to stand on Mount Gerizim for the purpose of blessing and on Mount Ebal for the curse (Deuteronomy 27:11). Ebal was the northern mountain and Gerizim was to the south. Shechem was located in the valley between the two mountains.

(2) It was at Shechem that Joshua is reported to have made his powerful speech to the ". . . elders, heads, the judges, and the officers of Israel," challenging them to be the people of Yahweh.

> . . . choose this day whom you will serve, whether the gods your fathers served in the region beyond the River, or the gods of the Amorites in whose land you dwell; but as for me and my house, we will serve Yahweh (Joshua 24:15).

(3) And of course, as we related in the previous chapter, it was to Shechem that Rehoboam, the son of Solomon, came to negotiate with *all Israel* concerning the future of his reign.

Shiloh

(1) Shiloh was the location of a temple of Yahweh in the pre-monarchical period (1 Samuel 1–2). In Jeremiah Yahweh is quoted as calling Shiloh

> . . . Shiloh . . . where I made my name dwell at first (Jeremiah 7:12).

And in Psalm 78, a Deuteronomist Psalm, we read:

> Shiloh, the tent where he dwelt among mortals (Psalm 78:60).

(2) Shiloh was the home of Samuel, a major prophet for the Deuteronomic circle:

> And all Israel from Dan to Beersheba knew that Samuel was a trustworthy prophet of the LORD. The LORD continued to appear at Shiloh, for the LORD revealed himself to Samuel at Shiloh by the word of the LORD. And the word of Samuel came to all Israel (1 Samuel 3:19–4:1).

We should note the use of the phrase *all Israel* used twice in the above passage. This was a common Deuteronomistic phrase to project the concept of unity into the circle's history of Israel's past.

(3) Shiloh was the home of Ahijah, the prophet who announced to Jeroboam that Yahweh would give him the ten northern tribes and establish his house (1 Kings 11:29–35).

Jeroboam's Break with Shechem and Shiloh

If anyone, Jeroboam is the villain of the Deuteronomistic history. Again and again the kings of Israel are criticized for continuing in the sins of Jeroboam. For example, of Jehoash who reigned for sixteen years (804–788) we read:

> He also did what was evil in the sight of the LORD; he did not depart from all the sins of Jeroboam son of Nebat, which caused Israel to sin, but walked in them[2] (2 Kings 13:11).

And of Ahab's marriage to Jezebel, an enemy of Yahweh and a champion of the Syrian Baal, we read:

> And as if it had been a light thing for him to walk in the sins of Jeroboam son of Nebat, he took as his wife Jezebel daughter of King Ethbaal of the Sidonians (1 Kings 16:31).

When Jeroboam was first accepted as king of the ten northern tribes we are informed that he "built Shechem." Immediately thereafter we are told that he moved from Shechem and "built Penuel." While no details are given here of an important break with the priesthood of Shechem, it is obvious that the move from Shechem was the beginning of Jeroboam's revolt against Yahweh, as seen by the Deuteronomists. Immediately after the move from Shechem we are told that Jeroboam established Bethel and Dan as official shrines of Israel, as competition for Jerusalem.

Then Jeroboam said to himself . . . If this people continue to
go up to offer sacrifices in the house of the LORD at Jerusalem, the heart of this people will turn again to their master,
King Rehoboam of Judah (1 Kings 12:27).

While we do not hear of any further detailed activity at Dan, we
know that Bethel became the major shrine in Israel (called the
king's sanctuary by Amaziah the priest in a story of Amos, 7:13) and
a target of the Deuteronomists, both in their history and in their
Josianic redaction of the books of Amos and Hosea. For example in
Amos we read:

On the day I punish Israel for his transgressions,
I will punish the altars of Bethel. . . .
For thus says the LORD to the house of Israel:
Seek me and live, but do not seek Bethel (Amos 3:14; 5:4–5).

In the history, one of the acts of Josiah which makes him the perfect
servant of Yahweh is his destruction of Bethel.

Moreover, the altar at Bethel, the high place erected by
Jeroboam son of Nebat, who caused Israel to sin—he (Josiah) pulled down that altar along with the high place. He
burned the high place, crushing it to dust[3] (2 Kings 23:15).

There is a fact which is likely to be overlooked in our discussion
of Bethel as a rival shrine to Jerusalem. The fact is that at its
inception Bethel was not only a rival shrine to Jerusalem, but also a
rival shrine to Shechem. Not only did Jeroboam move his capital
from Shechem, he also broke completely with the Levitical priests of
Shechem by creating a new priesthood.

. . . and he (Jeroboam) appointed priests from among the
people who were not Levites (1 Kings 12:31).

In a most unusual passage in DH we are told that a man of God from
Judah predicted the destruction of Bethel in the hearing of Jeroboam, by a son of the house of David, and the name of the destroyer
will be Josiah (1 Kings 13:1–2).

Even after this event Jeroboam did not turn from his evil
way, but made priests for the high places again from among

the people; any who wanted to be priests he consecrated for the high places. This matter became sin to the house of Jeroboam, so as to cut it off and to destroy it from the face of the earth (1 Kings 13:33–34).

Why Did Jeroboam Move Away from Shechem?

Facts concerning Jeroboam's move from Shechem are conspicuously absent. After Jeroboam became king this is all we are told concerning the move to Penuel, Israel's second capital:

> Then Jeroboam built Shechem in the hill country of Ephraim, and resided there; *he went out from there* and built Penuel (1 Kings 12:25).

One thing is certain. As soon as we are told that Jeroboam left Shechem we are immediately told that he established the shrines of Dan and Bethel, and that he appointed priests from among the people *who were not Levites.*

We are told that the shrines were nationalized as rival shrines to Jerusalem. As we mentioned above we are liable to miss in this account the obvious fact that national shrines of Jeroboam were not only rival shrines to Jerusalem, but they were rival shrines to Shechem.

In breaking with Shechem, Jeroboam also broke his Shiloh connection. Immediately after the second statement about creating a new priesthood,

> Jeroboam . . . made priests for the high places again from among the people; any who wanted to be priests he consecrated for the high places (1 Kings 13:33),

we are informed of Jeroboam's new, hostile relationship with Ahijah the prophet. In a story of the sickness of Jeroboam's son, he sends his wife to Shiloh to consult with Ahijah. She cannot reveal her identity however. Jeroboam is reported to have instructed her:

> Arise and disguise yourself, that it be not known that you are the wife of Jeroboam (1 Kings 14:2).

The above observations reveal to us an important characteristic of DH. In its history it is completely silent about its authors. The authors do not self-consciously provide us with any details concerning themselves, the circle of Levitical priests and scribes which produced DH. This is illustrated for us in the fact that Jeremiah, the outstanding prophet who was active during the reign of Josiah, and a vital player in Jerusalem politics during the last decades of Judah's existence, is not mentioned in the Deuteronomistic history. It is our contention that the absence of references to Jeremiah in the closing chapters of DH was a conscious decision of the school we call the Deuteronomists of which Jeremiah was a leading member. It is in accordance with this practice that we are not given details concerning the break with the Levitical priests of Shechem/Shiloh by Jeroboam, the first king of Israel. These Levitical priests were considered to be the ancestors of the Jerusalem authors of the Deuteronomistic history.

Since almost every king of Israel is accused of perpetuating the sins of Jeroboam, and therefore condemned, it is important to examine just what Jeroboam is accused of. He did not try to replace Yahweh with another God. When he established Bethel and Dan as national shrines he is reported to have referred to the exodus from Egypt.

> Here are your gods, O Israel, who brought you up out of the land of Egypt (1 Kings 12:28).

Many scholars have pointed out that the calf (bull) was not intended to be a symbol for Yahweh, but was recognized as a throne or pedestal for the invisible God.[4] In the *New Jerome Biblical Commentary* Jerome T. Walsh writes:

> . . . these figures (the calves) were not intended to represent the deity. Despite the words put in Jeroboam's mouth they were seats (or perhaps pedestals) for the invisible God enthroned upon them. Although the bull pedestal appears in the cult of Baal, Jeroboam clearly intends to establish sanctuaries of Yahweh.[5]

Much later, in a mature Judaism, Jeroboam's action would have been recognized as intolerable.[6] But at the time of the erection of the bull/pedestal, it was not considered outlandish.

Was the original sin of Jeroboam, as seen by the author of DH, the establishment of two shrines, instead of one? Hardly. After the original mention of Dan it is almost completely ignored and hardly mentioned again while all criticism is centered on the one shrine of Bethel, both in the Deuteronomistic history and in the Deuteronomistic editing of the two 8th century prophets Hosea and Amos.

Whatever was later understood and explained as the sin of Jeroboam, it is more likely that the original sin of Jeroboam was his break with the priests of Shechem (and the prophet of Shiloh, Ahijah). This is stated several times if we read carefully.

He (Jeroboam) also made houses on high places and appointed priests from among the people, who were not Levites (1 Kings 12:31).

Following the establishment of Bethel as an official altar, we encounter a story (folklore).[7] In an incident referred to above, we are told that while Jeroboam himself was offering incense[8] a prophet from Judah confronted him and predicted that a son of the house of David named Josiah would desecrate and destroy this altar. Jeroboam is said to have stretched out his hand with a command to seize the prophet.

But the hand that he (Jeroboam) stretched against him withered so that he could not draw it back to himself (1 Kings 13:4).

Later we read:

Even after this event Jeroboam did not turn from his evil way, but made priests for the high places again from among all the people; any who wanted to be priests he consecrated for the high places (1 Kings 13:33).[9]

What Was the Sin of Jeroboam?

In the Deuteronomistic history every king of Israel, the northern kingdom, is accused of walking in the ways of Jeroboam or not departing from the sins of Jeroboam. For example we read of a king named Zechariah:

He did not depart from the sins of Jeroboam son of Nebat,
which caused Israel to sin (2 Kings 15:9).

The above words are formulaic, and with the passage of time formulas become stereotypes. In this chapter we are suggesting that the *sins of Jeroboam* originally consisted of more than the establishment of Bethel and Dan as national shrines with calf images. We will reconstruct what happened following the death of Solomon.

The Levitical priesthood of Shechem, in addition to being zealous advocates of Yahweh, had a strong social agenda. It is for this reason that Rehoboam, the son of Solomon, came to Shechem to be made king of Israel. The Shechemites were responsible for uniting the farmers and citizens of Israel in a rebellion against the unfair, abusive economic policies of Solomon, heavy taxation to support the monarchy and forced labor (*corvee*). With popular support they forced Rehoboam to come to their territory, Shechem, to negotiate with the people. When Rehoboam refused to negotiate, the Shechemite priesthood supported Jeroboam as an alternative monarch. Following his becoming king however, Jeroboam decided that he was not willing to reign under the domination of the Levite social agenda and moved the capital from Shechem to Penuel. We have pointed out that one of the marks of DH is that the authors do not call great attention to themselves or their activities. So we only find a slight reference to the break between Jeroboam and the Levites.

> . . . he (Jeroboam) went out from there (Shechem) and built Penuel (1 Kings 12:25).[10]

This was a rejection of the Levitical priesthood by Jeroboam, and several times later we read of Jeroboam appointing priests who were not Levites for his shrines (1 Kings 12:31 and 13:33).

It is not unreasonable to suggest that the first sin of Jeroboam, before the setting up of the calf images at Bethel and Dan, was his break with the priests of Shechem, the ancestors of the authors of DH, and his break with their social agenda. We also pointed out that his actions caused a rift between him and the prophet of Shiloh who had first declared his monarchy, Ahijah. This circle continued at Shechem without official sanction and produced the anti-monarchical material reported in Samuel (1 Samuel 8:10–22 for example).

Centuries later in Jerusalem, this relocated priesthood, or at least a circle of priests, scribes and prophets who considered themselves the legitimate descendants of the Shechem priesthood, would re-examine the role of the monarchy for Judah's (Israel's) survival. They now lived in a changed political, economic and social environment. Their view of the ancient monarchy was altered and they came to see support for the house of David as Israel's best chance for political survival in a world of international military and political threat. They were able to produce a view of history which could distinguish between a good king and a bad king, depending on the relationship of the monarch to Yahweh, the ancient God of Israel, for whom they were his most zealous champions.

Deuteronomic Central Reform Goal in the Days of Josiah

The goal of the Deuteronomic circle was the centralization and standardization of the cult of Yahweh in Jerusalem. In the past the place which Yahweh chose to make his name dwell may have been Shechem or Shiloh, but during the reign of Josiah the place chosen by Yahweh was Jerusalem. Cultic purity was the chief concern of the Deuteronomists. This meant the purging of all practices considered by the circle to be Canaanite or Assyrian. Although Bethel was an ancient Canaanite and Israelite shrine, with a long Israelite tradition, as a competing shrine, Bethel had to be discredited and destroyed. The Deuteronomists would have liked to blame all the deviations of Bethel on Jeroboam:

> The people of Israel continued in all the sins that Jeroboam committed; they did not depart from them until the LORD removed Israel out of his sight (2 Kings 17:22–23).

Not all the practices of Bethel could be traced to Jeroboam however. Following the destruction of Israel in 722, not only were the chief citizens of Samaria carried into captivity, but a relocated population from the east was placed in Israel by the Assyrians.[11] In an interesting account, we are told that because these relocated people did not know how to worship Yahweh, "the LORD sent lions among them which killed some of them" (2 Kings 17:25). The Assyrians decided to remedy this situation by sending an Israelite priest to Bethel:

> So one of the priests whom they (the Assyrians) had carried away from Samaria came and lived in Bethel; he taught them how to worship the LORD. . . . So they worshiped the LORD but also served their own gods, after the manner of

the nations from among whom they had been carried away.
To this day they continue to practice their former customs
(2 Kings 17:28,33).

To This Day

In conjunction with this discussion of foreign worship in Bethel
we encounter the very interesting phrase *to this day*.

To this day they continue to practice their former customs
(2 Kings 17:34).

The expression *to this day* appears repeatedly in DH, and is one of
the indications which informs us that the first edition of the
Deuteronomistic history appeared before the destruction of Judah
by the Babylonians, *after which the expression would have been
inappropriate.*[12]

Before we turn to the many parallels between Joshua, who begins the history, and Josiah, who ended the first edition, we will list
five examples of verses which contain the expression *to this day*.

(1) This verse speaks of the Gibeonites who were allowed to
become hewers of wood and drawers of water.

(They became) hewers of wood and drawers of water for the
congregation and for the altar of the LORD, to continue to
this day (Joshua 9:27).

(2) This verse speaks about the Jebusites of Jerusalem whom
the people of Judah did not drive out of Jerusalem.

. . . so the Jebusites live with the people of Jerusalem to this
day (Joshua 16:63).

(3) This verse mentions an ancient tradition which granted the
town Ziklag to David.

. . . therefore Ziklag has belonged to the kings of Judah to
this day (1 Samuel 27:6).

(4) This verse mentions the poles which were attached to the
ark. They were long.

The poles were so long that the ends of the poles were seen
from the holy place in front of the inner sanctuary . . . they
are there to this day (1 Kings 8:8).

(5) This verse speaks of foreigners who were not driven out of
the land.

Their descendants who were left in the land . . . these Solomon conscripted for slave labor, and they are there to this
day (1 Kings 9:21).

While the above five referenced verses may indicate that the
first edition of DH appeared while Judah was still in existence,
scholars during the last two decades have been able to identify the
exact time that the first edition of DH made its appearance. It appeared during the reign of Josiah to support and celebrate his reformation activity.[13]

NOTES

1.   See Map »1. Also note on the map the proximity of Bethel
to Jerusalem.

2.   *To walk* in the ways of the LORD is a common Deuteronomic expression. Here it is used negatively, *to walk* in the sins of
Jeroboam.

3.   This expression *crushing it to dust* is also used in Deuteronomy 9:21 where Moses destroys the golden calf made by Aaron.

4.   See the article on 1 Kings by John Wevers in *The Inter-
preter's One Volume Bible Commentary*, page 191.

5.   See page 169 of *The New Jerome Biblical Commentary*.

6.   The exilic Deuteronomists were so successful in their fight
against the use of images that it is almost impossible for the beginning Bible student to see the action of Jeroboam in erecting the
calves as anything but an obvious betrayal of Israel's deepest religious foundations. Actually, when Jeroboam erected the calves his

action was almost normal. We have no record of the people of Israel finding anything strange about it.

7.   In our first chapter we distinguished between history, story, and theology. Story often involves a confrontation between a prophet and a king. See for example the reported confrontation between Elijah and Ahab in 1 Kings 21:17–29.

8.   Gale Yee in her book *Composition and Tradition in the Book of Hosea* points out that the use of incense particularly irritated the Deuteronomists. See Hosea 4:13 and 11:2.

9.   There is an interesting conflict here. On the one hand we are told that Jeroboam established two official shrines. On the other hand we are informed that he encouraged worship at the high places. One explanation is that the author was referring to Bethel and Dan as the high places. We should keep in mind that the account we are reading is from the viewpoint of the 7th century Deuteronomist.

10.   From Penuel the capital was moved to Tizrah, seven miles northeast of Shechem. Eventually the house of Omri purchased and built Mount Samaria as the capital of Israel

11.   See 2 Kings 17:24.

12.   There are some scholars who do not feel that the expression "to this day" is an indication of pre-exilic authorship, but that the expression appeared in the original sources and was allowed to remain there. See for example Richard Nelson in *Double Redaction*, page 23.

13.   These are four of the chief works to be consulted which identify Josiah as the king in whose reign the first edition of DH appeared. Frank Moore Cross, *Canaanite Myth and Hebrew Epic* (Cambridge: Harvard University Press, 1973). Richard Elliot Friedman, *The Exile and Biblical Narrative*, Harvard Semitic Monographs (Chico: Scholars Press, 1981). R. D. Nelson, *The Double Redaction of the Deuteronomistic History* (Sheffield: JSOT Press, 1981). Andrew D. H. Mayes, *The Story of Israel between Settlement and Exile* (London: SCM Press, 1983).

Chapter 4

JOSHUA AND JOSIAH

Throughout the Deuteronomistic history (DH) there is an assessment of each king's reign. We mentioned that all the kings of the northern kingdom were condemned for walking in the sins of Jeroboam. Many of the Judean kings are also condemned for not walking in the ways of David, allowing worship at the high places, and participating in Canaanite and foreign worship practices. These assessments tend to conform to a formula.

One of the first things for us to notice is that in the canonical edition (final edition) of DH the formula for the assessment of the four kings following Josiah differs from the assessment formula for the previous kings of Judah. Josiah and the kings before him were often compared with David. For example, of Ahaz it is recorded:

> He did not do what was right in the sight of the LORD his God, as his ancestor David had done (2 Kings 16:2).

Not only are the kings *after* Josiah not compared with David, but after the death of Josiah there is no mention of the name of David at all. Scholars believe that the material in 2 Kings following the reign of Josiah was added some time after the termination of the house of David (during the exile or later). This material is part of a later, second edition or exilic edition of DH.

Also there is no condemnation of the high places in the assessment formula for the kings following Josiah. But the high places continued to exist after Josiah (Jeremiah 17:1–3). Perhaps the most interesting aspect of the formula can be seen in the remarks made about Jehoahaz and Jehoiakim, the two kings who followed Josiah.

He (they) did what was evil in the sight of the LORD just as
all his (their) ancestors had done (2 Kings 23:32 and 36).

Whoever wrote these words ignored the great reformation of Josiah
and the righteousness attributed to him, as if Josiah had never lived.

But the overriding reason for identifying the culmination of the
first important edition of DH with Josiah are the many parallels
between Joshua, who begins the history, and Josiah who ends (the
first edition of) the history. Friedman writes, "The literary evidence . . . points to a full stop. . . . Josiah is more than important. His
reign is the literary focus of the work."[1] We note that both Josiah
and Joshua read from the book of the law to the people. The book
which Josiah receives has the same title as the book which Joshua
receives, *sepher hatorah*. Both leaders sponsor a national passover.
Both lead a reform to put aside all practices related to the worship of
foreign gods. Both may be said to have led covenant renewal ceremonies. Josiah is the only king (in fact the only person) to whom the
words of Joshua are applied concerning not turning *to the right or to
the left*. Both are warriors. Josiah follows Joshua's command to turn
to the LORD with all his heart and with all his soul by keeping the
laws of Moses. (See our chart #2.)

Who Was Joshua?

Before the appearance of the first edition of DH Joshua was an
obscure Ephraimite hero. Michael David Coogan writing in the *New
Jerome Biblical Commentary* says:

> . . . the most that can be said is that Joshua was an Ephra-
> imite, perhaps a local hero who became the focus for the
> idealized reconstruction of early Israel in Dtr (DH).[2]

In the present arrangement of the books of the Hebrew Bible, after
the book of Joshua he disappears completely except for several references in the book of Judges. Joshua is completely unknown in the
prophets, major or minor. His name and deeds are never mentioned.
Joshua served the historian as a literary device. Norman Gottwald
theorizes that ". . . the accounts of two (military) thrusts by the
Ephraimite Joshua, one into Judah and the other into Galilee," was
a concession to the northern and southern tribal groups.[3]

Richard Nelson in his dissertation *The Double Redaction of the*

CHART 2
PARALLELS BETWEEN JOSIAH AND JOSHUA

JOSIAH   **JOSHUA**

1. Both read from the book of the law to the people.

   2 Kings 23:2   Joshua 8:34–35

2. The book which Josiah receives has the same title in Hebrew as the book which Joshua receives, book of the law, *sepher hatorah.*

   2 Kings 22:8, 11   Joshua 1:8; 8:31, 34

3. Both sponsor a national passover.

   2 Kings 23:21–23   Joshua 5:10

4. Both lead a reform to put aside foreign gods.

   2 Kings 23:5–14   Joshua 23:14–16, 24:20

5. Both lead public covenant renewal ceremonies.

   2 Kings 23:3   Joshua 24:22–28

6. Josiah is the only king to which the words of Joshua are applied concerning not turning *to the right or to the left.*

   2 Kings 22:2   Joshua 23:6

7. Josiah follows Joshua's command to turn to the LORD with all his (your) heart and all his (your) soul, by keeping the laws of Moses. Of no other king are these words used.

   2 Kings 23:25   Joshua 22:5

Deuteronomistic History states that Joshua was the creation of the historian, patterned after King Josiah.

> Indeed, the pre-Deuteronomistic Joshua tradition contained only the element of military leadership among all those listed; the rest were added to his character by the historian himself. In other words, much of our present picture of Joshua is nothing but a retrojection of the figure of Josiah into the classical past.[4]

What we have in the first edition of DH is a bracketing of the entire history with an elaborate account of the perfect hero of Yahweh, setting forth first Joshua, and later Josiah. The activity of each hero sets forth the theological values held by the Deuteronomists during the reign of Josiah. (See our chart »2, Parallels Between Josiah and Joshua.)

The picture of Josiah is further heightened in the telling of the discovery of the book of the law. His attitude is compared with the two men who made the discovery, the priest Hilkiah and the scribe Shaphan. Their reaction to the discovery is told in a routine fashion, and their reporting of the discovery of the book to Josiah is presented as an afterthought while they are reporting to him on the progress of the temple repairs. The response of Josiah however is anything but mundane.

> When the king heard the words of the book of the law, he tore his clothes . . . for great is the wrath of the LORD that is kindled against us (2 Kings 22:11–13).

What all this means, these parallels between Joshua and Josiah, is that the person of Joshua belongs to story (folklore) and theology, rather than to history. Also, the Israel which Joshua leads is also folklore, the continued epic of twelve families belonging to twelve sons of one man, Jacob (Israel). Many scholars, including Martin Noth, have suggested that the boundary divisions appearing in the book of Joshua for the tribes date from the administrative organization of Josiah.[5]

Who Was Josiah?

The account of Josiah's temple repairs and his religious reforms is so exciting that the student is apt to ignore the question of the historicity of the account. The reasoning follows this line of thought. Joshua lived centuries ago, so his story may be a work of literary art. But the Josiah account was written while he was alive, so it had to be true. Not all scholars agree however.[6]

The first crack in the Josiah account appears in the book of Chronicles. In Kings we are told that the discovery of the book of the law initiated the great religious reforms of Josiah. In Chronicles however we are told that the religious reforms were well under way when "the book of the law of the LORD given through Moses" was discovered (2 Chronicles 34).[7]

Another scholar, Andrew Mayes, in his commentary on Deuteronomy raises doubt about Josiah's temple repairs, suggesting that the repair of the temple is based on an earlier incident related in 2 Kings 12:1–16. Mayes suggests that the temple repair program became part of the Josiah account to provide "a historically credible context for the story of the finding of the book of the law."[8] Also, Joseph Blenkensopp in his commentary on Deuteronomy in *The New Jerome Biblical Commentary* raises the possibility that the account of Josiah's temple restoration and the discovery of the book of the law may be "a free composition of the Deuteronomists."[9]

The information supplied for us concerning the reign of Josiah in DH exceeds information supplied for the other kings of Judah with the possible exception of Hezekiah.[10]

The account of Josiah's reign as we have it is very well crafted. Only when we break down its elements do we realize how much is included in only two chapters:

1. Temple repair program.
2. Discovery of the book of the law, the torah.
3. Huldah's two-part prophecy.
4. Reading the book of the law to the people.
5. Leading the people in covenant renewal.
6. Cleansing the temple and defiling the high places.
7. Bethel is destroyed and defiled.
8. High places in Samaria are destroyed.
9. A national passover is held in Jerusalem.
10. There are further reforms (mediums, idols, etc.).
11. Josiah is killed in battle at Megiddo.

In our chart of *Parallels Between Josiah and Joshua*, it may be objected that we had a long account of Joshua (24 chapters) to search for parallels. In our defense there are two things which can said:

(1) The book of Joshua which we now have is longer than the book of Joshua which appeared in the Josianic edition of DH. (We will discuss this in our next chapter devoted to the levels of authorship in DH, and in chapters 7 and 8 where we discuss the exilic edition of DH.)

(2) The reason so much is compressed into the account of Josiah is because of its nature. It was composed to serve as the grand finale of the entire history.

Assyrian Power Fading

The mention of Josiah's incursion into Samaria (2 Kings 23:19) is important because it provides us with information concerning the international balance of power which made possible the heightened nationalism underlying the Deuteronomic reforms.

Samaria (renamed Samarina by the Assyrians) was and had been for a century a province of Assyria. Assyrian power, which had dominated Judah and her neighbors in the Palestine-Syria area for three centuries, was in the process of final collapse. The Chaldeans from the southeast, whom we know as Neo-Babylonians, were emerging as the new, world military power in Mesopotamia. The famous Assyrian King Ashurbanipal died in 627, and the occasion of his death triggered rebellion throughout the Assyrian empire, including the small nation of Judah and her neighbors. In 625, only four years before the reform program of Josiah, Nabopolasser gained control of Babylon and established the Neo-Babylonian empire. These are the circumstances which enabled Judah to experience a renewed nationalism tied closely to religious reforms and the theological innovations of the Deuteronomists.

A Major Parallel

There is a parallel between Joshua's activity and Josiah's activity to which we should pay special attention. That special correspondence is found in the role of *the people*. In much of DH, the role of the people in the survival of Israel and Judah is not clear. Again and again the reason for Israel's destruction is centered on the sins of Jeroboam and the kings who followed him. As far as the southern kingdom is concerned, we are told that the survival of Judah depended on a promise from Yahweh to David, a covenant between two individuals, Yahweh and David. In the account of the secession of the northern tribes from Judah, previously discussed in our chapter 2, we are told:

> One tribe (Judah) will remain his (Rehoboam's), for the sake of my servant David and for the sake of Jerusalem, the city that I have chosen (1 Kings 11:32).

Later in the account of Hezekiah we read:

> I will defend this city for my own sake and for my servant David's sake (2 Kings 20:6).

Also, in the original 8th century oracles of the prophets Hosea, Amos, and Micah, the destruction of Samaria and Jerusalem is predicted because of the acts of the king and the representatives of the king, the elite decision makers of Samaria and Jerusalem. The *role of the people* in the survival of Israel and Judah is not clear.

In Joshua however, and in the account of Josiah, the role of the people looms large. A relationship is referred to that is not between Joshua and Yahweh, or Josiah and Yahweh, but between the people of Israel and Yahweh.

> Then *the people* answered, "Far be it from us that we should forsake the LORD to serve other gods (Joshua 24:16).

> The king (Josiah) went up to the house of the LORD, and all the people went with him. . . . All the people joined in the covenant (2 Kings 23:1–3).

The very real possibility exists that if the account of Joshua is more theological than historical, then the account of Josiah may also be more theological than historical. In order to explore this real possibility it is necessary for us to become acquainted with the stages of the development of DH.

The Last Verse of the Josianic Edition of DH

In our next chapter we will introduce the four layers of authorship of DH. We will also continue to examine the content and characteristics of the two main editions, Josianic and exilic. This may be the closing verse of the Josianic edition:

Moreover Josiah put away the mediums and the wizards and the teraphim and the idols and all the abominations that were in the land of Judah and in Jerusalem, that he might establish the words of the law which were written in the book that Hilkiah the priest found in the house of the LORD (2 Kings 23:24).[11]

NOTES

1. Friedman, *The Exile and Biblical Narrative*, page 7.

2. See article on Joshua in *New Jerome Biblical Commentary*, page 111.

3. Norman Gottwald, *The Tribes of Yahweh*, page 178. The entire Part IV concerning Joshua and Judges in *Tribes* is highly recommended reading.

4. Richard Nelson, *The Double Redaction of the Deuteronomic History*, page 125.

5. Noth, *History of Pentateuchal Traditions,* pages 273ff.

6. Even today in an age of mass communication, it is difficult if not impossible to obtain an accurate account of the actions of persons in public life, even the president of the United States. A negative example is the work of Joseph McGuiness in his book entitled *The Selling of the President*, which demonstrated how much misinformation was distributed during a presidential campaign. The public view of the candidate depends not on demonstrated facts but on the work of professional press agents. All I am suggesting is that information concerning a living person can be fiction also.

7. An interesting idea is presented in a book by Giovanni Garbini entitled *History and Ideology in Ancient Israel* concerning the parallels between Josiah and Joshua. Garbini says there are more comparisons between Joshua and Josiah of Chronicles, whom he calls the *priestly* Josiah, than the Josiah of DH. See page 130.

8.   See A.D.H. Mayes, *The New Century Bible Commentary, Deuteronomy* (Grand Rapids: Eerdmans, 1991), page 91.

9.   See page 95 of *NJBC*.

10.   Hezekiah is also recognized as a reformer who loved Yahweh and during whose reign centralization was attempted. Also the Hezekiah account is long because it covers the siege of Jerusalem by Sennacherib in 701.

11.   There is no agreement among scholars as to whether verse 24 (of 2 Kings 23) is the last verse of the Josianic edition. There are good reasons to believe that the account of the Josianic reign was worked over by an exilic editor. A.D.H. Mayes says that 2 Kings 23:25 was the final verse, but others say that the words in verse 25, ". . . who turned to the LORD," are exilic. Also the closing words of verse 25, ". . . nor did any like him arise after him," were exilic additions. Some scholars believe that verse 23 may be the closing verse of the Josianic edition.

Chapter 5

THE FOUR LAYERS OF AUTHORSHIP
OF THE DEUTERONOMISTIC HISTORY

In this book we will refer to the books of Joshua, Judges, Samuel, and Kings[1] as the Deuteronomistic history (DH). In a later chapter we will discuss the book of Deuteronomy as "The Prologue."

The first edition which we discuss will be called the Josianic edition. As we explained in chapter 4, this edition started with Joshua and ended with Josiah. We are not calling it the first edition because there is always the possibility that generations before Josiah, the same group of Levitical priests which traced its heritage to the northern cities of Shechem and Shiloh started to compile this history, even as early as the reign of Hezekiah.[2]

Whether this earlier effort ever had exposure outside the Levitical priestly circle we do not know. The first really important edition of DH appeared during the reign of Josiah. It interpreted the history of Israel/Judah, from the entering of the land, in the light of a profound and highly organized theology. It ended up being a string of epic sermons. It had two purposes:

(1) It explained why Yahweh had allowed the northern kingdom of Israel to be destroyed by the Assyrians in 722.

(2) It explained why Yahweh had allowed Judah to survive, and what Judah had to do to continue receiving Yahweh's blessing.

The Primary Sources

The primary sources were both official (monarchic records) and non-official (priestly or prophetic traditions). We can only speculate

46

CHART 3
FOUR LAYERS OF AUTHORSHIP OF THE
DEUTERONOMISTIC HISTORY

1. **Primary Sources** (See chart 4).
2. **Josianic Edition,** completed before the destruction of Jerusalem, late 7th century.
3. **Exilic Edition,** a redactional expansion of the Josianic edition, composed middle or late 6th century.
4. **Canonical Edition** (5th century).

---

as to why and how all these primary sources were available to the authors of DH.

(1) The Levitical priesthood of Shechem may have preserved manuscripts of its own, some dating from before the tragedy of 722, and others written in Judah based on oral traditions of the north. If this were so, and it is highly possible, then they may have been able to make an arrangement with those who controlled Jerusalem sources, for a mutual lending and borrowing agreement, or at least for an opportunity to make copies of each other's scrolls.

(2) The author(s) of DH may have had good relations with the ruling class in Jerusalem, or have been a member of the ruling class.

At any rate it is safe to say that only in Jerusalem could many of the sources listed below have been available. Some sources are referred to, such as the Book of Jashar (Joshua 10:13), while other sources are produced almost in their entirety, such as the court history of David (2 Samuel 9–20; 1 Kings 1–2). The historian informs the reader that he is only using selected material from his sources by frequent announcements such as:

> Now the rest of the acts of Elah, and all that he did, are they not written in the book of the Annals of the Kings of Israel (1 Kings 16:14)?

It is necessary to keep in mind the fact that not one of these primary sources is available to us today apart from their appearance in DH. Here is a brief summary of the story which the historian told.

Using the sources cited above, and perhaps others not men-

CHART 4
PRIMARY SOURCES USED BY THE AUTHORS OF THE DEUTERONOMISTIC HISTORY

1. Song of Deborah, an ancient divine warrior hymn (Judges 5).
2. Boundary, territory, and city lists (Joshua 13–22).
3. List of judges (10:1–5; 12:7–15).
4. Stories of ancient deliverers (throughout Judges).
5. Book of Yashar (Joshua 10:13; 2 Samuel 1:18).
6. List of top fighters (2 Samuel 23:8–39).
7. Stories of the sacred ark (1 Samuel 4:1b–7:1).
8. Court history of David; the succession narrative (2 Samuel 9–20; 1 Kings 1–2).
9. Book of the Acts of Solomon (1 Kings 11:41).
10. Chronicles of the kings of Israel (1 Kings 14:19).
11. Chronicles of the kings of Judah (1 Kings 14:29).
12. Cycle of Elijah stories.
13. Cycle of Elisha stories.
14. Military sources.
15. Hymn of Yahweh's unique governance (1 Samuel 2–10).
16. Historical traditions from various locations.
17. Other sources and fragments, named and unnamed.
18. Prophetic traditions.

---

tioned, the historian started the story of Israel with conquest of the land under the leadership of Joshua, and the division of the land among the tribes. After Joshua's death, the unity of Israel fades as a factor as Yahweh raises hero deliverers to rescue groups within Israel. These heroes are linked uncomfortably with judges who rule areas of Israel. Samuel is a prophet, judge and teacher supreme. He is a bridge between the period of the judges and the first two kings, Saul and David. David captures Jerusalem and makes it the capital of Israel. David receives a divine message from Yahweh, through the prophet Nathan, declaring that his house will endure forever.

The united kingdom splits after the death of Solomon, and the historian tells us of the kings in the north (Israel) and the kings of the south (Judah), chronologically interlocking their reigns. The northern kingdom is destroyed by Assyria in 722 because the kings of Israel followed the sins of Jeroboam. Judah survives however, and a century later the historian praises Josiah's efforts to restore the kingdom of the house of David. Even the north will be reunited with Judah as in days of old. This history covers a period of 600 years.

Josianic Edition of the Deuteronomistic History

The Josianic edition of DH was shorter than the version which now appears in our Bible. We can only speculate on its exact length. Here are eleven facts about the *Josianic edition* of DH with which we should be familiar. Some of these facts will help us to contrast the Josianic version with the later, exilic edition of DH.

(1) The first edition was optimistic in that it both started and ended with perfect and obedient servants of Yahweh, Joshua and Josiah.

(2) Each division of the Josianic edition of DH (Joshua, Judges, Samuel, Kings) was shorter than the version which now appears in our Bible (the canonical edition).

(3) The complete conquest of the promised land was stated.[3]

(4) The fate of the nation (Israel and Judah) depended largely on the behavior of the king.

(5) It promoted the centralization and standardization of the worship of Yahweh in Jerusalem.

(6) It criticized the kings of Judah for not removing the high places.

(7) It championed the house of David, and contrasted the survival of the house of David with the dynasties of the northern kingdom.

(8) It told of the destruction and desecration of the shrine at Bethel by Josiah.

(9) It contained many key roles for prophets emphasizing the important use of prophets by Yahweh in the history of Israel.

(10) Speeches were scattered throughout the Josianic version of DH, sometimes attributed to heroes and great persons, and other times appearing as summaries by the historian himself.

(11) The *Name theology* is characteristic of the Josianic historian (see below).

In the remainder of this chapter we will comment on some of eleven items in the above list. Other items in the list will be discussed in following chapters, where we will examine the exilic edition of DH.

The Complete Conquest

The student must become aware that there are two versions of the conquest of the promised land in the canonical edition of DH. One presents the conquest as complete (Joshua 21:43–45). The other view tells us that the so called *conquest* was gradual, and anything but complete (for example, Judges, chapter 1).

In Joshua 21:43–44 we read:

Thus the LORD gave Israel all the land that he swore to their ancestors that he would give them; and having taken possession of it, they settled there. And the LORD gave them rest on every side just as he had sworn to their ancestors; not one of all their enemies had withstood them (Joshua 21:43–44).

And further in Joshua 11:23 we read:

So Joshua took the whole land according to all that the LORD had spoken to Moses; and Joshua gave it for an inheritance to Israel according to their tribal allotments. And the land had rest from war (Joshua 11:23).

This view of complete conquest is reversed in Judges, chapter 1, where we are told again and again, that the tribes did not drive out the inhabitants of the land:

Manasseh did not drive out the inhabitants of Bethshean (v. 27).
Ephraim did not drive out the Canaanites who lived in Gezer (v. 29).
Zebulun did not drive out the inhabitants of Kitron (v. 30).
Asher did not drive out the inhabitants of Acco (v. 31).
Naphtali did not drive out the inhabitants of Bethshemesh (v. 33).

We do not have to depend on Judges for this correction of the complete conquest viewpoint. In Joshua 23 there are several verses which speak of the nations which remain among you.[4]

It is our belief that in the first edition of DH, the Josianic historian purposely over-simplified the conquest period, presenting a complete conquest, in accordance with his optimistic presentation, to gain united support for Josiah's reforms and to promote the annexation of the northern territory.[5] Josiah was in the process of annexing Samarina (an Assyrian province), the former territory of Israel.

Other Josianic Elements in the Pre-Exilic Version of DH

In addition to the complete conquest, we must become familiar with other elements of the pre-exilic edition of DH. For example, we believe that the account of the destruction and desecration of the shrine at Bethel was part of the Josianic edition also. It was an essential move in the centralization decision, and is in accordance with editorial activity of the Deuteronomists and their redaction of the oracles of two 8th century prophets, Amos and Hosea, performed during the reign of Josiah. We will discuss this in greater detail in our chapter 11.

In the Josianic edition we are told that Israel (the north) was destroyed because the kings all perpetuated the sins of Jeroboam. The kings of Judah are criticized for not removing the high places, which provided a series of local competitive shrines to Jerusalem, but Josiah was going to correct this situation.[6] The role of the people in the destruction of Israel was not clear in the early edition of DH.

Mixed Feeling About the Monarchy

As part of its optimistic outlook, the Josianic edition of DH stressed the unconditional promise made by Yahweh through the prophet Nathan to David and the house of David:

> Your house and your kingdom shall be made sure forever before me; your throne shall be established forever. In accordance with all these words and with all this vision, Nathan spoke with David (2 Samuel 6:16).

In spite of this acceptance and promotion of the unconditional promise to the house of David, scholars have long pointed out an uncomfortable mixture of pro-monarchical and anti-monarchical material throughout the book of 1 Samuel. We believe that the early, Josianic edition could well have contained both pro- and anti-monarchical traditions.

If the Deuteronomists were indeed the inheritors of the Shechem Levitical priestly views, as we are suggesting, then there is no doubt that they brought with them to Jerusalem, following the tragic events of 722, a strong anti-monarchical tradition from the north. Although these traditions were carefully preserved by the displaced circle of northerners, a hundred years went by before the book of the law was discovered in the temple. In the course of a hundred years attitudes can and do change. When we meet these Levites through their scrolls we discover that their attitude concerning the role of the monarchy, specifically the house of David, has changed. As time went by they had decided that the best way to perpetuate the cult of Yahweh and to insure its survival was to promote the house of David, particularly in the person of Josiah, a son of the house of David.

The historian had at his disposal both anti- and pro-monarchical traditions.[7] In the light of a long Shechemite anti-monarchic tradition, and the change in attitude toward the house of David, the historian made a decision to harmonize both anti- and pro-monarchical traditions. In doing so, he produced an ambiguous picture.[8] This is not the only reason for the ambiguity however. It is possible that further anti-monarchical material was added to the later, canonical version, long after the destruction of Jerusalem in 587/6.

The Name Theology

Then Solomon said,
"The LORD has said that he would dwell in thick darkness.
I have built you an exalted house, a place for you to dwell in
    forever" (1 Kings 8:12–13).

The above words, attributed to Solomon at the time of the dedication of the temple which he built, represent a popular, ancient Jerusalem tradition. This anthropomorphic theology (thinking of God in human terms) associated with the idea that the God of Israel would desire and have pleasure in a special *dwelling place* is typical of the theology of a Jerusalem priesthood known as the Aaronide priesthood.[9] Because of the popularity and well established antiquity of this tradition[10] (Yahweh dwelling in the temple), the Josianic historian included it in his edition of DH. However he immediately followed this passage with an extended Deuteronomic statement explaining the correct, Deuteronomic belief concerning God's relationship to the temple.

The Name theology means that the LORD does not dwell in the temple (or Jerusalem) but only his name dwells there. Near the beginning of the Deuteronomic torah we read this:

> . . . you shall seek the place that the LORD your God will choose out of all your tribes as his habitation *to put his name there* (Deuteronomy 12:5).

The Josianic historian in his account of the dedication of the temple made his point repeatedly (5 times) in the next paragraph by repeated reference to the Name theology:

> . . . that my name might be there (1 Kings 8:16).
> . . . a house for the name of the LORD (8:17).
> . . . a house for my name (8:18).
> . . . the house of my name (8:19).
> . . . and have built the house for the name of the LORD (8:20).

In the event that the reader (hearer) missed the point, and still conceived of the LORD as dwelling in the temple, instead of *his name* dwelling in the temple, the historian wrote this explanation:

> But will God indeed dwell on the earth? Even heaven and the highest heaven cannot contain you, much less this house that I have built (1 Kings 8:27).

The *Name theology* is the work of the Josianic historian. The exilic editor did not use the name theology.[11]

The Death of Josiah

The sudden and unexpected death of King Josiah came as a shock to the Deuteronomists. In the optimistic history which they had produced, Josiah was the culmination of a long series of events, the beginning of a bright age, a new era of justice and righteousness for the people of Yahweh. And then:

> In his days, Pharaoh Neco king of Egypt went up to the king
> of Assyria to the river Euphrates. King Josiah went to meet
> him; but when Pharaoh Neco met him at Meggido, he killed
> him. His servants carried him dead in a chariot from
> Meggido, brought him to Jerusalem, and buried him in his
> own tomb (2 Kings 23:29–30).

We don't know how long it took for the full impact of this shock to take its toll on the circle of scribes and priests who produced the first edition of DH. As was their practice, autobiographical information is lacking. We do know that the nationalistic reformation of Josiah came to an abrupt halt. In less than three months, Judah became a vassal of Egypt. Josiah's son Jehoahaz was carried to Egyptian captivity from which he never returned. Then Pharaoh appointed another son of Josiah as king.

> Pharaoh Neco made Eliakim son of Josiah king in place of
> his father Josiah and changed his name to Jehoiakim (2
> Kings 23:34).

This fact, and other information which we have of the history of Judah after Josiah, was added much later by another author. All the news is bad. Judah was overrun by enemies. By 597 the Chaldeans, whom we know as neo-Babylonians, had defeated the Egyptians and had taken command of Jerusalem. Nebuchadnezzar carried away into Babylonian captivity the chief citizens of Jerusalem.

> The king of Babylon . . . carried off all the treasures of the
> house of the LORD, and the treasures of the king's
> house. . . . He carried away all Jerusalem, all the warriors,
> ten thousand captives, all the artisans and the smiths; no
> one remained except the poorest people of the land (2
> Kings 24:12–14).

Eleven years later the temple of the LORD and all the chief houses of Jerusalem were burnt to the ground and the walls of the city were leveled. More citizens were carried away into captivity, while others fled to Egypt and elsewhere.

These events, beginning with the sudden death of Josiah, had rendered the first edition of the Deuteronomistic history (DH) irrelevant and inconsequential. The first edition of DH had set out to

---

CHART 5
ELEVEN FACTS ABOUT THE JOSIANIC EDITION
OF THE DEUTERONOMISTIC HISTORY

(1) The first edition was optimistic in that it both started and ended with perfect and obedient servants of Yahweh, Joshua and Josiah.

(2) Each division of the Josianic edition of DH (Joshua, Judges, Samuel, Kings) was shorter than the version which now appears in our Bible (the canonical edition).

(3) The complete conquest of the promised land was stated.

(4) The fate of the nation (Israel and Judah) depended largely on the behavior of the king.

(5) It promoted the centralization and standardization of the worship of Yahweh in Jerusalem.

(6) It criticized the kings of Judah for not removing the high places.

(7) It championed the house of David, and contrasted the survival of the house of David with the dynasties of the northern kingdom.

(8) It told of the destruction and desecration of the shrine at Bethel by Josiah.

(9) It contained many key roles for prophets emphasizing the important use of prophets by Yahweh in the history of Israel.

(10) Speeches were scattered throughout the Josianic version of DH, sometimes attributed to heroes and great persons, and other times appearing as summaries by the historian himself.

(11) The *Name theology* is characteristic of the Josianic historian.

---

answer the question, "Why had Yahweh allowed the Assyrians to destroy the northern kingdom of Israel, and why had Yahweh allowed Judah to survive?" In the light of events following the death of Josiah, DH was in need of a complete updating and revision. It had to deal with new, deeply disturbing theological developments which had not been imagined by the authors of the Josianic edition.

NOTES

1. In some Bibles Samuel and Kings are called 1 Kings, 2 Kings, 3 Kings, and 4 Kings. We will be using the arrangement in the New Revised Standard Version: 1 Samuel, 2 Samuel, 1 Kings, 2 Kings.

2. Since there may have been a pre-Josianic edition of the history, technically speaking that would be the first edition. What public exposure this pre-Josianic history had, if any, is unknown to us. To discuss it in this book would be counter-productive.

3. The view that the Josianic edition contained only the complete conquest viewpoint is thoroughly developed and explained in the important study by A.D.H. Mayes, *Israel Between Settlement and Exile*. See the chapter on Joshua, the opening pages of the chapter on Samuel, pages 82–83, and the Conclusion, pages 133–134.

4. See Joshua 23:4, 7, and 11. Richard Nelson identifies these verses as exilic additions to the final speech of Joshua 23. Joshua 24 has another origin which we will discuss elsewhere.

5. Frank M. Cross in *Canaanite Myth and Hebrew Epic* (Cambridge: Harvard Press, 1973) explains how the Josianic edition served as a platform for Josiah's hopes to restore northern allegiance to Jerusalem and the house of David, pages 284ff.

6. We are not sure what responsibility the people had in using the high places in the pre-exilic edition of DH. There is no doubt that in the canonical (final) edition of DH, the people of both Israel and Judah are severely criticized. In the Josianic edition responsibility is centered on the behavior of kings. See the comments concerning Ahaz in 2 Kings 16, or the typical comment made about Azariah of Judah, ". . . the high places were not taken away." We will discuss the responsibility of the people in our chapters 7 and 8.

7. For an example of an anti-monarchic tradition read the speech attributed to Samuel in 1 Samuel 8:11–18. For an example of pro-monarchic material read 1 Samuel 9:15–17 and 1 Samuel 10:20–27.

8.   Scholars have always pointed out passages in 1 Samuel which are pro-monarchical and anti-monarchical. There is no doubt that two traditions are preserved and that there was an attempt to harmonize these two viewpoints.

9.   There are many scholarly works which describe the anthropomorphic (human-like) attributes of God reflected in the scriptures of the Aaronid priesthood. The priestly documents are part of the first four books of the canonical Bible, the tetrateuch (Genesis, Exodus, Leviticus, Numbers). In many ways these scriptures picture the LORD as dwelling in the midst of the people. Moshe Weinfeld writes in *Deuteronomy and the Deuteronomic School* (page 197), "Indeed all sacral activity performed in the tabernacle as described by the priestly writings is, as we have pointed out, based on the assumption of God's actual immanence in the sanctuary."

10.   The words ascribed to Solomon which begin this section (1 Kings 8:12–13) may have been part of a popular liturgy. The historian started teaching his viewpoint, the *Name theology*, by quoting a verse familiar to the readers (listeners).

11.   Richard Friedman, in his book *The Exile and Biblical Narrative*, calls the historian DTR 1. He states ". . . the Deuteronomistic Name theology . . . occurs only in DTR 1 passages. See page 11 in his book.

Chapter 6

THE DEATH OF JOSIAH

The death of Josiah was a tragedy of immense proportions for Jerusalem and Judah, and for the Deuteronomists who had made Josiah the hero of their movement and the culmination of their history (DH).

The Bible student reading the book of 2 Kings receives no descriptive detail concerning the chaos and turmoil in Jerusalem caused by the death of Josiah. Not a hint of the immense confusion and disarray is portrayed. Events are reported (such as the burial of Josiah) as if they were everyday occurrences. Formulaic language is used.

There were several reasons for this:

(a) The account of Josiah's death (and the aborted three-month reign of his son, Jehoahaz), was added to the Josianic edition of the Deuteronomistic history, many years after the events recorded.

(b) Events which followed in the next two decades, including the complete destruction of Jerusalem and the temple by the neo-Babylonians (Chaldeans) overshadowed the tragic dimensions of these earlier events.

(c) Egypt was the enemy of Judah at the time that Josiah was killed, but allegiances in days following shifted back and forth. At the time that the account of Egypt's takeover was added (2 Kings 23), it may have been in the best interest of the editor to downplay the destructive activity of Egypt toward Judah at the end of the 7th century.

What Happened in the Circle of the Deuteronomists?

As we have pointed out several times it was the practice of the circle to keep accounts of their internal affairs apart from the history which they produced. For this reason they had not supplied us

58

CHART 6
FINAL KINGS OF JUDAH

NAME	DATES	LENGTH OF REIGN	INFORMATION
JOSIAH	640–609	31 Years	Killed in battle at Megiddo by Pharaoh Neco.
JEHOAHAZ	609	3 Months	Taken as a prisoner to Egypt where he died.
JEHOIAKIM	609–598	11 Years	Began his reign as an Egyptian vassal.
JEHOIAKIN	597	3 Months	Taken into Babylonian captivity by Nebuchadnezzar.
ZEDEKIAH	597–586	11 Years	Blinded and carried into Babylonian captivity.
GEDALIAH (Governor at Riblah)	585	7 Months	Assassinated by Judean nationalists.

with details concerning their ancestral split with Jeroboam, the first
king of Israel, at Shechem; nor did they report on the activity of
Jeremiah who was a member, if not the leader of the circle, during
the days of Josiah.

One thing became clear as the years passed. The theological purpose of the Josianic edition of DH was rendered irrelevant and obsolete. The historical content of the history and the collected folklore
would continue to be a national treasure of immense value, but the
theological structure would have to be reworked. One of the original
goals of the Josianic edition of DH was to explain why Judah had
survived with Yahweh's blessing (as the north did not survive), and
how Judah could continue to flourish. Josiah was the personification
of the perfect servant of Yahweh as was Joshua. The history supported
the centralization and standardization of the cult of Yahweh in Jerusalem. The disorder following Josiah's death and the subjection of Judah as a vassal, first to Egypt and then to Babylon, changed the rules
of the game. The final blow to the relevancy of the theological viewpoint of the Josianic edition of DH took place in the tragic events of
587/6 when the Babylonians destroyed Jerusalem and the temple,
and carried another large group of Judeans into Babylonian captivity.

The Historian and the Editor

Some scholars refer to the author of the Josianic edition of DH
as the historian, and the person or persons who edited and enlarged
DH during the exilic period (producing an enlarged Joshua, Judges,
Samuel, and Kings *almost* as we have them today) as the editor.
However, in this chapter, and for the remainder of this book, we will
not simply refer to the two as the historian and the editor. Rather, to
assist the reader in keeping the different circumstances and perspec-
tives in mind, we will often refer to them as the *Josianic* historian
and the *exilic* editor.

This does produce a small problem. When the word *exilic* is
used, we are apt to think of the Babylonian experience. Some scholars have suggested however that the exilic edition of DH was not
produced in the Babylonian community.

Where Was the Exilic Version of the
Deuteronomistic History Produced?

We do not know where the editors (or editor) of DH were located
when they made their great revisions. Many assume that the com-

munity of Judahites in Babylon was the logical location. But we know that there was a Judahite community in Egypt (Jeremiah 43:6–7) following the final destruction of Jerusalem. Jeremiah and Baruch his scribe were included in this number against their will. We also know that many of the rural poor remained behind in Judah. We also have reason to believe that other groups of Judahites sought refuge in other countries of the near east.

Some scholars suggest the possibility that the exilic edition was produced in Egypt.[1] It is a commonplace to say that during the exile the ancient exodus tradition was revised and renewed to reach the foundational position of centrality which it now occupies in the Hebrew Bible. We immediately realize that the people of Yahweh in Babylon would see the parallels and would read "Babylon" for Egypt in their present circumstances. It is good to keep in mind, however, that for some Judeans, Egypt literally meant Egypt. Concluding a description of curses in Deuteronomy we find these words:

> The LORD will bring you back in ships[2] to Egypt, by a route that I promised you would never see again; and there you shall offer yourselves for sale to your enemies as male and female slaves, but there will be no buyer (Deuteronomy 28:68).

If Jeremiah, Baruch, and their devotees continued the work of the Deuteronomists, which is possible, then Egypt would have been the location of the exilic edition.

Why Did Yahweh Allow Judah To Be Destroyed? An Early Answer

The unexpected death of Josiah and the immediate fall of Judah, first as a vassal of Egypt, then as a vassal of Babylon, presented a severe theological problem for the Josianic historian and the Deuteronomists. Josiah had been the culmination of a long history, and his program of religious reforms was meant to signal the beginning of a great new age for Israel. What went wrong to cause the wrath of Yahweh to break out in such fury that the nation of his people came to such a heartbreaking and humiliating end? An early answer, added to the Josianic edition of DH, looked to the reign of Manasseh for an answer.

> Before him (Josiah) there was no king like him, who turned
> to the LORD with all his heart, with all his soul, and with
> all his might.... Still the LORD did not turn from the
> fierceness of his great wrath, by which his anger was kin-
> dled against Judah, because of all the provocations with
> which Manasseh had provoked him (2 Kings 23:25–26).

In order to understand this unsatisfying answer, we have to examine
the description of the reign of Manasseh in 2 Kings 23.

Manasseh reigned for 55 years. In 2 Kings his reign is covered in
18 verses, and no significant historical information is included apart
from the opening and closing formulas for the kings of Judah (his age,
his mother's name, his burial place). Although 55 years is a long time,
the only thing the historian decided to tell us is that Manasseh was an
evil villain (redundancy intended). By the time the Josianic historian
reached the reign of Manasseh, he either had lost interest in historical detail, or he was anxious to get to Josiah, the hero of the work.
Beginning in verse 2 of chapter 23, and continuing through verse 9,
the historian listed the religious sins of Manasseh. It has always been
obvious to scholars that all the acts of Manasseh are forbidden in the
opening words of the Deuteronomic torah (Deuteronomy 12), and that
each of his crimes was corrected by the acts and reforms of Josiah.

Perhaps the historian ignored historical facts of Manasseh's 55
year reign so as not to distract us from his theological purpose. The
picture of Manasseh was meant to be as evil as the portraying of
Josiah was meant to be righteous. The contrast served to heighten
Josiah's goodness.[3]

Shortly thereafter, when the people of Yahweh found themselves defeated and scattered, with Judah destroyed, an exilic editor
came up with an early explanation which was not inconsistent with
the theology of the Josianic historian. If the northern kingdom had
been destroyed in 722 because of the sins of Jeroboam (and the kings
who followed him), then Judah could have been destroyed because of
the sins of her kings. Josiah had been obedient, but the crimes of
Manasseh weighed too heavily in the scales of justice, and Yahweh
had to punish Judah. So the following verses were added to the
Josianic account of Manasseh's reign:

> The LORD said by his servants the prophets, "Because
> King Manasseh of Judah has committed these abomina-
> tions, has done things more wicked than all that the Amo-
> rites did, who were before him, and has caused Judah to sin

---

CHART 7
THE JOSIANIC EDITION OF THE
DEUTERONOMISTIC HISTORY

The first collection of scrolls recognized as a revelation of
Yahweh appeared during the reign of Josiah, 640–609 B.C.E.*

Contents

PROLOGUE	Parts of the Deuteronomic torah (chapters 12–13 and portions of other chapters through 26) with a narrative introduction linking Moses with the torah, followed by rudimentary blessings and curses.
History of Israel following Moses' farewell address and death	The first history of Israel starting with Joshua and ending with Josiah, called the Josianic edition of DH (Joshua, Judges, Samuel, Kings).
POSTLUDE	A four-part liturgical scroll based on the oracles of four 8th century prophets: Hosea, Amos, Isaiah, Micah.

* Before the appearance of the collection referred to here
several scrolls existed with limited circulation. These sources
are called by scholars J, E, and P. Following the exile, during
the period of rebuilding and restoration, these sources were
expertly blended together (including some D material) to form
a tetrateuch (Genesis, Exodus, Leviticus, Numbers) and were
placed before our Prologue, Deuteronomy.

---

with his idols; therefore thus says the LORD the God of
Israel, I am bringing upon Jerusalem and upon Judah such
evil that the ears of everyone who hears of it shall tingle" (2
Kings 21:10–12).

Believing that the extent of Manasseh's evil overrode and cancelled
the obedience of Josiah was a simplistic and unsatisfying answer. It

may also have been unhistorical. A century later the author of Chronicles using a different source about Manasseh informs us that before he died Manasseh repented before Yahweh, and conducted vast reforms himself.

> He (Manasseh) took away the foreign gods and the idol from the house of the LORD, and all the altars he had built on the mountain of the house of the LORD and in Jerusalem, and threw them out of the city. He also restored the altar of the LORD and offered on it sacrifices of well-being and of thanksgiving; and he commanded Judah to serve the LORD the God of Israel (2 Chronicles 33:15–16).

By reading the above we discover that the author of Chronicles did not blame the sins of Manasseh for the destruction of Jerusalem. Blaming Manasseh proved to be unsatisfying to those who continued the school of the Deuteronomists. After they regained their balance and reviewed aspects of their emerging theology, they realized that blaming an evil individual for the fate of a nation excluded an essential factor in the theology which was developing in their midst. That essential factor was the role of the people, the role of *all Israel*, and the relationship of the people to Yahweh. After the monarchy was destroyed and rendered helpless it became clear to the Deuteronomists that a relationship between Yahweh and the people was more important than the relationship between Yahweh and the house of David. It was at this point of realization that the concept of a covenant between Yahweh and the people, in the form of a vassal treaty, emerged as an explanation of the complete history of Israel. It was back to the drawing board for a complete revision of the Josianic edition of the Deuteronomistic history.

NOTES

1. See Friedman's monograph entitled *The Exile and Biblical Narrative*, pages 35–36.

2. The meaning of the words "in ships" is obscure. But it is important to note that the return to Egypt is voluntary in that the Israelites will offer themselves as male and female slaves but will not be hired.

3.   An interesting parallel is found in a modern mystery story written by Josephine Tey, *The Daughter of Time* (New York: Macmillan, 1953). In this book a Scotland Yard inspector conducts an investigation from his hospital bed of the villainy of Richard III. He discovers that Richard III (a member of the house of Plantagenet) may have been purposely vilified by a history commissioned by the Tudors to make them look better. Shakespeare later based his play *Richard III* on this biased history.

Part II

Chapter 7

THE EXILIC EDITION OF THE
DEUTERONOMISTIC HISTORY

In this chapter we will further define and identify the contents of the Josianic edition of DH by examining and discussing changes and additions made to the first three sections, Joshua, Judges, and Samuel, following the destruction of Jerusalem and the temple, in the period called the exile. (We will discuss the books of Kings in chapter 8.)

With some degree of confidence we can reconstruct the Josianic edition of DH, but there are associated questions which we cannot answer. These questions include such mundane matters as to the number of copies which existed and how they were used.

We can safely speculate that the reason for producing DH and updated versions of the four 8th century prophets was didactic. In order to reach the goal of centralization and standardization, *the people* of Judah had to be educated. The scrolls were not produced for scholars, or for the shelves of libraries. Since a limited number of scrolls could be produced, and since reading was not widespread, we can assume that public reading was the chief goal of scroll production.

We are told of public readings of the torah by Joshua (Joshua 8:35), Josiah (2 Kings 23:2), and later by Ezra (Nehemiah 8). In the Josianic editions of the prophetic books (see our chapter 11) we find liturgical responses and the use of hymnic material which indicate public participation and ceremony.[1]

While we believe that the Josianic historian produced DH for the purpose of public readings, what we can't be sure of is this: Were these public readings instituted before the untimely death of King Josiah?

69

And we do not know how many copies existed at that time also. It is possible that only one copy of the Josianic edition of DH existed and that this copy was carried to Egypt by Jeremiah and Baruch.[2] But this is only speculation on our part. A copy or copies may have been carried to Babylon also. Would it have been possible for Jeremiah and Baruch to have produced the exilic edition of DH?[3] The answer to this question is obviously yes.[4] Jeremiah and Baruch were in the right places at the right times, and they certainly were skilled enough and concerned enough to do the job.

While we may never be able to say with complete assurance that the exilic edition of DH was produced in Babylon or Egypt, and whether it was the work of Jeremiah and Baruch (or their heirs and followers), there are many important things we can know concerning the important exilic edition of DH, and the ways it changed the earlier, Josianic version.

References to the Scattering of the People

References to the threat of exile are found throughout the final version of DH. Scholars are cautious about assigning all exilic threats and predictions of exile to the exilic editor. Exile was a common practice of the Assyrians, and long before the death of Josiah and the rapid decline of Judah, the people and their spiritual leaders were quite familiar with the fate of Israel in 722.

But there is much agreement that certain exilic passages were edited into the text after the fact. We have already mentioned (chapter 6) that after the enumeration of Manasseh's religious crimes in 2 Kings 21:1–10, an editor added verses 10–15, including these words:

> I will cast off the remnant of my heritage, and give them into the hand of their enemies; they shall become a prey and a spoil to all their enemies (2 Kings 21:14).

And also this paragraph was added:

> Still the LORD did not turn from the fierceness of his great wrath . . . because of all the provocations with which Manasseh had provoked him. The LORD said, "I will remove Judah also out of my sight, as I have removed Israel; and I will reject this city that I have chosen, Jerusalem, and the house of which I said, My name shall be there" (2 Kings 23:26–27).

Earlier in DH, at the conclusion of a passage explaining the reason for Israel's fall (the northern kingdom) this exilic passage appears:

> Judah also did not keep the commandments of the LORD their God but walked in the customs that Israel had introduced. The LORD rejected all the descendants; he punished them and gave them into the hand of plunderers, until he had banished them from his presence (2 Kings 17:19–20).

Almost all scholars assign the following words from Yahweh to Solomon (at the conclusion of his prayer dedicating the temple) as an exilic passage:[5]

> . . . then I will cut Israel off from the land that I have given them; and the house that I have consecrated for my name I will cast out of my sight, and Israel will become a heap of ruins; everyone passing by it will say, "Why has the LORD done such a thing to this land and to this house" (1 Kings 9:7–9).

It is easy to identify exilic additions to DH, but it is more profitable for us to examine the editing of DH section by section to assist us in understanding the breadth of the exilic theology which replaced the simpler theology of the Josianic edition. In this chapter we will cite examples of editorial expansion and reconstruction in the first three sections of DH, Joshua, Judges, and Samuel.

Joshua[6]

> And now I am about to go the way of all the earth, and you know in your hearts and souls, all of you, that not one thing has failed of all the good things that the LORD your God promised concerning you; all have come to pass for you, not one of them has failed (Joshua 23:14).

These are the last words of the Josianic version of the book of Joshua. The words complete a farewell address attributed to Joshua. This address will end the period of conquest and begin the period of the judges.[7] The words of Joshua's farewell speech are fitting for the optimistic and hopeful purposes of the historian. (The negative passage which follows, and the entire last chapter, 24, were not part of

the Josianic edition.[8]) The above words are in harmony with other
summaries which appeared earlier in the Josianic version:

> So Joshua took the whole land, according to all that the
> LORD had spoken to Moses; and Joshua gave it for an in-
> heritance to Israel according to their tribal allotments. And
> the land had rest from war (Joshua 11:23).

And later we read:

> And the LORD gave them rest on every side just as he had
> sworn to their ancestors; not one of all their enemies had
> withstood them, for the LORD had given all their enemies
> into their hands (Joshua 21:44).

The Josianic edition of Joshua was divided into two parts. First
Joshua conquered the land (1–11), then he divided the land among
the tribes of Israel (12–23).[9] It presented a view of complete conquest, with an ideal Israel and an ideal leader. This view paralleled
the peace and good times of the Josianic era. Decades later, when the
circumstances of the people of Yahweh had changed as completely as
imaginable, following the devastation of Jerusalem and the temple,
and the carrying away of the Judahites into captivity, an exilic editor (or editors) decided to introduce a different view of the ancient
settlement of Israel. In the closing speech of Joshua, for example,
three references were added to "the nations left here among you"
(verses 4, 7, 12).[10] Another passage which was added to the exilic
edition appears in chapter 13:

> Now Joshua was old and advanced in years; and the LORD
> said to him, "You are old and advanced in years, and very
> much of the land still remains to be possessed" (Joshua
> 13:1).

And in Judges chapter 1 (another exilic addition) we will find detailed information concerning the people of Canaan who were not
displaced.

    Why did the exilic author change the picture? Did he add this
information because of the acquisition of an additional primary
source? Perhaps he felt that the picture of the people of Yahweh
living side by side with worshipers of strange gods in ancient times
mirrored the circumstances in which they now found themselves in

Babylon and Egypt. Perhaps the answer to our question depends on our understanding of the purpose of the exilic edition of DH. In the Josianic edition, Jerusalem and Judah were preserved because of the unconditional promise of the LORD to David through the prophet Nathan (2 Samuel 7). The theological question which the exilic edition had to answer was this: Why had the LORD allowed Jerusalem and the temple and the people to be so thoroughly devastated? The answer would be built on the preoccupation of the Deuteronomists with (1) cultic purity and (2) obedience to the laws of Yahweh, teachings which began to surface in the didactic purpose of the Josianic edition, but which did not reach their mature, structured form until the exilic period. We will discuss this in greater detail below.

In chapter 2 we distinguished between three kinds of material found in DH, theology, history, and folklore (or story). The material in Joshua, the battle of Jericho (chapter 6)[11] and the sun standing still in the sky (chapter 10) have to be viewed as story, rather than history. We should not let these stories distract us from the major fiction of the book however which is the unity of the Israel which Joshua is said to have addressed in chapter 23, and, later, in chapter 24. Norman Gottwald has referred to the unity of Israel in the book of Joshua as ". . . convenient fiction."[12] The expression *all Israel* which appears again and again in DH projects a unity on ancient Israel which certainly could not have existed.[13]

The question which we face is not whether this farewell address (chapter 23) is an authentic speech of Joshua. It is not. The historical Joshua lived at least 600 years earlier, and the authors of DH knew little or nothing about him. The question which we must answer is this: Which part of the speech *attributed to Joshua* is Josianic (written before the destruction of Jerusalem) and which part is exilic (a time when Israel was devastated and scattered, the 6th century). Although there is not complete agreement among scholars concerning the content of the Josianic and the exilic version of these books, Joshua, Judges, Samuel, and Kings, we will cite some of the most obvious examples as we continue. For example, consider how appropriate these words, appearing in the opening chapter of Joshua, would be for *scattered Israel* after the destruction of Judah:

> This book of the law shall not depart from out of your mouth; you shall meditate on it day and night. . . . Be strong and courageous; do not be frightened or dismayed, for the LORD your God is with you wherever you go (Joshua 1:8–9).

Judges

The material in the book of Judges moves us from the settlement of Israel in the land toward establishment of the monarchy by
uncomfortably combining stories of ancient heroes with lists of
judges. The hero/deliverers are brought together with judges in
Judges 2:11–23.

> Then the LORD raised up judges, who delivered them out of
> the power of those who plundered them (Judges 2:16).

The ancient heroes responded to temporary emergencies in particular locations, whereas the judges served for life. In the list of
judges found in 10:1–5 and 12:7–15, only one delivering hero is
mentioned, Jephthah.[14]
The first verse of the Josianic version of Judges was chapter 2:6:

> When Joshua dismissed the people, the Israelites all went
> to their own inheritances to take possession of the land
> (Judges 2:6).

This verse set the scene for the book of Judges where, as scholars
have noted, the concept of a united Israel (referred to throughout DH
by the Deuteronomic expression *all Israel*) just about fades completely. The concept of unity will make its appearance again early in
the book of 1 Samuel:

> And *all Israel* from Dan to Beersheba knew that Samuel
> was a trustworthy prophet of the LORD (1 Samuel 3:20).

The Josianic edition of Judges had continued the *complete conquest* picture. For this reason, in the Josianic edition of Judges, the
enemies of Israel are from outside their borders, the Ammonites, the
Philistines, and the Midianites. The exilic editor added chapter 1 of
Judges, which dispels the *complete* conquest concept with significant
detail (read verses 27–34), and the story of an angel's warning in
chapter 2:1–5, which also dispels the complete conquest picture.
Some scholars believe that a primary source was a scroll of
ancient heroes. If this is true, then the book of Judges will hold
particular interest for students who want to understand the values
of ancient, pre-monarchic Israel. Judges contains more ancient
source material than the book of Joshua, which revealed more about

the Josianic age and the exilic age (the ages in which it was written) than ancient times.

The Four-Part Pattern

There is a four-part pattern (sin-punishment-repentance-deliverance) repeated again and again in the book of Judges with which all readers are familiar. A clear example of this pattern is found in Judges 3:7–11.[15]

> (a) "The Israelites did what was evil in the sight of the LORD" (verse 7).
> (b) "The anger of the LORD was kindled against Israel" (verse 8).
> (c) ". . . the Israelites cried out to the LORD" (verse 9).
> (d) "the LORD raised up a deliverer for Israel . . . the land had rest" (verses 9 and 11).

It is possible that this obvious pattern (stated and re-stated many times) may not have been part of the Josianic edition. In the Josianic edition these ancient stories (primary sources) may only have served the purpose of moving the history of the people forward to the days of Samuel when the monarchy was established. It is important to note that in the four-part pattern of Judges (sin, punishment, repentance, deliverance), the punishment comes from Yahweh as a result of the behavior *of the people*. In the exilic edition, this pattern may have been superimposed on the Josianic edition of Judges. It blames the people of Yahweh for the terrible situation in which they find themselves, and gives them hope, encouraging them to ". . . cry to the LORD," who in times past sent salvation and restored rest to the land.

Whether the four-part pattern was part of the Josianic edition of DH or whether it was superimposed on ancient material during the exile is an interesting subject for further study. While Josiah was still alive, the goal of the Deuteronomists to centralize and standardize the cult of Yahweh in Jerusalem included the didactic purpose of teaching the people their responsibility to know and keep the law. The opening of the Deuteronomic torah dealt with matters of cultic purity.

This does not mean that there was an understanding of a covenantal relationship based on a vassal treaty form before the death of

Josiah however. In a monumental work on DH,[16] *Israel Between Settlement and Exile*, Andrew Hayes states that all references to covenant theology (between Yahweh and the people of Israel) made their appearance in the exilic edition of DH, and that covenant theology (at least that form of covenant theology based on the vassal treaty form) was not part of the thinking of the Josianic historian of DH.[17] For this reason he assigns references to the covenant between Yahweh *and the people* (not the covenant between Yahweh and David) to the exilic editor. For example:

> So the anger of the LORD was kindled against Israel; and he said, "Because this people have transgressed my covenant that I commanded their ancestors, and have not obeyed my voice, I will no longer drive out before them any of the nations that Joshua left when he died (Judges 2:20–21).

We will discuss the various meanings of the word covenant as they are found in the Hebrew Bible in our chapter 9, "The Origin of Covenant Theology."

Samuel (1 and 2)

The four sections of DH (Joshua, Judges, Samuel, Kings) do not possess the same characteristics. It is reasonable to believe that traditions concerning the early monarchy far outnumbered traditions of earlier times. And the availability of sources influenced the nature of each section of DH.

The two books of Samuel, with the three formidable characters, Samuel the Ephraimite, Saul the Benjaminite, and David the Judahite, bring the age of the judges to an end (1 Samuel 12) and begin the account of the monarchy in Israel. Primary sources were plentiful for the historian, including blocks, such as stories of the sacred ark (1 Samuel 4:1–7:1), which do not mention Samuel, and the court history, the first part of the so-called succession history (2 Samuel 9–20).[18] Doublets, or two different explanations or versions of the same event, appear throughout the Hebrew Bible, but the books of Samuel contain some of the most obvious.

There are at least two versions of the selection of Saul as king, two versions of the rejection of Saul as king, two versions of the introduction of David to Saul, two accounts of David sparing Saul's

```
┌─────────────────────────────────────────────────────┐
│                      CHART 8                         │
│      EXAMPLES OF DOUBLETS IN THE BOOKS OF SAMUEL      │
│                                                      │
│  SAUL IDENTIFIED AS THE ONE SELECTED TO BE KING      │
│      1 Samuel          1 Samuel 10:17–21             │
│      9:15–17                                         │
│                                                      │
│  REASON FOR SAUL'S REJECTION                         │
│      1 Samuel          1 Samuel 15:10–34             │
│      13:9–14                                         │
│                                                      │
│  DAVID'S INTRODUCTION TO SAUL                        │
│      1 Samuel          1 Samuel 17:55–58             │
│      16:14–23                                        │
│                                                      │
│  ORIGIN OF THE PROVERB, "IS SAUL ALSO AMONG THE      │
│  PROPHETS?"                                          │
│      1 Samuel          1 Samuel 19:24                │
│      10:12                                           │
│                                                      │
│  DAVID SPARES SAUL'S LIFE WHILE SAUL IS SLEEPING     │
│      1 Samuel 24       1 Samuel 26                   │
│                                                      │
│  TWO ACCOUNTS OF SAUL'S DEATH                        │
│      1 Samuel 31       2 Samuel 1:1–10               │
│                                                      │
│  NAME OF PERSON WHO SLEW GOLIATH THE GITTITE         │
│      1 Samuel 17       2 Samuel 21:19                │
└─────────────────────────────────────────────────────┘
```

life while Saul was sleeping, two accounts of Saul's death, and two explanations of the origin of the proverb, "Is Saul also among the prophets?"

Before the production of DH there were many oral traditions tied to specific locations (local traditions) in pre-monarchic and monarchic Israel. It may have been that the historian, whose ancestors were from the north, decided to include both a northern version and a southern (Judean) version of the events in Samuel, producing the doublets referred to above.

Anti-Monarchic and Pro-Monarchic Viewpoints

The hand of an exilic editor is not widespread in the books of Samuel. It is profitable for us, however, to examine the mixing of pro- and anti-monarchic viewpoints expressed in 1 Samuel. The pericope below can only be read as pro-monarchic:

> Samuel said to all the people, "Do you see the one whom the LORD has chosen? There is no one like him in all the people." And all the people shouted "Long live the king!"
> Samuel told all the people the rights and duties of the kingship and wrote them in a book and laid it up before the LORD. . . . Saul also went to his home at Gibeah and with him went warriors whose hearts God had touched. But some worthless fellows said "How can this man save us?" (1 Samuel 10:24–27).

On the other side, the following three verses equate *the demand for a king* with rejection of Yahweh:

> And the LORD said to Samuel, ". . . they have not rejected you, they have rejected me" (1 Samuel 8:7).

> But today you have rejected your God who saves you from all your calamities (1 Samuel 10:19).

> . . . the wickedness that you have done in the sight of the LORD is great in demanding a king for yourself (1 Samuel 12:17).

The great German scholar Wellhausen stated that the anti-monarchic sections of Samuel were exilic or post-exilic and reflected both the disenchantment with the monarchy and the fact that the monarchy no longer existed. Recent scholars have reversed that view, stating that at least some of the anti-monarchic material had to be ancient. Our view is that the forerunners of the Deutero-nomists had a long anti-monarchic tradition. This anti-monarchic attitude was the natural outcome of the relationship between the Levites of Shechem and the monarchs of Israel (beginning with the split with Jeroboam) and was fostered by the continuation of the Levites as an unofficial, anti-establishment society.

But by the reign of Josiah, a hundred years had passed since the

Levitical priests of Shechem had fled south to Judah. As time passed, the circle's anti-monarchic view underwent a change. The decision was made that supporting the house of David (in the person of Josiah) was the best way to promote the survival of the cult of Yahweh and promote the general welfare.

To put it another way, the Deuteronomists were pro-monarchic with a strong anti-monarchic heritage. When the historian put together the Josianic edition of DH the decision was made to use both the northern anti-monarchic traditions and the pro-monarchic traditions of Judah and to harmonize the traditions. For better or for worse, ambiguity was the result. It is possible that this ambiguity may have been increased by exilic or post-exilic redaction.

Because of the nature of exilic editorial activity in the books of Kings, we will devote a chapter to a discussion of this activity.

NOTES

1. See a fine discussion of this subject in Chapter 3 of *New Paths Through the Old Testament*, by Carroll Stuhlmueller (Mahwah: Paulist Press, 1989). Also, examples are cited in my book *Isaiah of Jerusalem* (1992).

2. Read the paragraph "From Egypt to Egypt" in Richard Friedman's popular book, *Who Wrote the Bible?* pages 143–144.

3. At the time of Jeremiah's abduction to Egypt he was in his mid-fifties. We are told in Jeremiah, chapter 1, that he was called to be a prophet in the 13th year of Josiah's reign (627 B.C.E.) and that at that time Jeremiah was ". . . only a boy." Jeremiah could have been less than 55 years old in 585, the year of his abduction to Egypt.

4. See the book, *Who Wrote the Bible?* by Friedman, pages 146–149.

5. It is ironic that this devastating passage follows a passage where the LORD informs Solomon of the following promise:

I have heard your prayer and your plea, which you made before me; I have consecrated this house that you have

built, and put my name there forever; my eyes and my
heart will be there for all time (1 Kings 9:3).

Why didn't the editor change this passage? We believe that it was
the practice of the exilic editor not to omit words which were previously contained in the scroll he was editing. We will discuss this
principle later in this book.

6. An excellent commentary on the book of Joshua by Michael David Coogan is found in *The New Jerome Biblical Commentary* (Englewood Cliffs: Prentice-Hall, 1990), pages 110–131.

7. In 1 Samuel, Samuel will also make a farewell address to
mark the end of the period of judges and the beginning of the period
of the monarchy:

Samuel said to all Israel . . . I am old and gray but my sons
are with you (1 Samuel 12:1–2).

8   In Joshua 23, Joshua is about to die and is giving a farewell
speech, but in chapter 24 he is at the height of his powers. Chapter
24 is identified by scholars as a Shechem source added later to the
scroll of Joshua during the exile (or even later), including Moshe
Weinfeld, Richard Nelson, and A.D.H. Mayes. Also consult the commentary by Michael David Coogan in *The New Jerome Biblical Commentary,* pages 130–131.

9.   Some scholars believe that the divisions and boundaries in
Joshua dated from the Davidic-Solomonic period, and others from
the Josianic period.

10.   Both Richard Nelson and Andrew Mayes cite these three
verses (Joshua 23:4, 7, 12) as exilic. See Bibliography.

11.   Archeological conclusions indicate that Jericho was not in-
habited at the time of Joshua. For an introduction to archeology see
chapter 3 of *Reading the Old Testament* by Lawrence Boadt. Also see
pages 200–203. For a complete introduction to biblical archeology
consult section 74 of the *New Jerome Biblical Commentary* by Philip
J. King, pages 1196–1218. For information concerning Jericho, see
paragraphs numbered 79–80.

12. Norman Gottwald, *The Hebrew Bible, A Social-Literary Introduction*, page 252.

13. See the book by Robert Coote, *Early Israel, A New Horizon* (Minneapolis: Augsburg-Fortress, 1990), pages 1–7.

14. A.D.H. Mayes, *Israel Between Settlement and Exile*, page 63.

15. Some scholars divide the pattern into 6 steps (sin, punishment, call for help, raising up of the judge, victory and peace. See page 377 of *Reading the Old Testament* by Lawrence Boadt.

16. A.D.H. Mayes, *The Story of Israel Between Settlement and Exile* (London: SCM Press, 1983).

17. In our chapter 9, "The Origin of Covenant Theology" we will explain the difference between the covenant between David and Yahweh (not based on the vassal treaty form) and the covenant between Israel and Yahweh which *was based* on the vassal treaty form.

18. The block of material called the court history, or succession narrative (1 Samuel 9–20 and 2 Samuel 1–2) has been much studied. For a short summary of recent interpretation see Norman Gottwald's *The Hebrew Bible, A Socio-Literary Introduction*, pages 317–318.

Chapter 8

THE EXILIC EDITION OF THE DEUTERONOMISTIC HISTORY (CONTINUED)

Kings (1 and 2)

Early in the book of 1 Kings, the LORD appeared to Solomon twice. The first appearance was in a dream at Gibeon (1 Kings 3:5). At that time Solomon was granted wisdom by the LORD. This appearance is obviously based on an ancient popular tradition. The Josianic historian of DH repeatedly included popular traditions to meet the people where they were. Because the original source is ancient, Gibeon is recognized and mentioned as *the principal high place* ". . . where Solomon used to offer a thousand burnt offerings," without criticism. The Josianic historian was selective in his use of original sources, but once selected, the text would not be changed. A reason justifying the use of the high place is entered into the narrative by stating that the temple had not yet been built (verse 2).

The second appearance of the LORD to Solomon (1 Kings 9:2), following the completion of the temple, contains a passage which reveals the hand of the exilic editor. Almost all scholars assign the following words from Yahweh to Solomon as an exilic passage:[1]

> . . . then I will cut Israel[2] off from the land that I have given them; and the house that I have consecrated for my name I will cast out of my sight, and Israel will become a heap of ruins; everyone passing by it will say, "Why has the LORD done such a thing to this land and to this house?" (1 Kings 9:7–9).

Notice the use of the figure of people passing by the ruins and asking a question, "Why has the LORD done such a thing to this land?" A similar question appears in Deuteronomy 29, a passage which scholars identify as exilic.[3]

> . . . yes, all the nations will say, "Why has the LORD done thus to this land" (Deuteronomy 29:24)?

Smooth Transition to Abrupt Transition

In the narrative of 1 Kings, chapter 9, there are three layers of authorship.

(1) The promise to Solomon that the temple will be there for all time (v. 3) comes from original source material.

(2) The section of the narrative dealing with the establishment of the dynasty of the house of David (v. 5) is the work of the Josianic historian, supporting the kingship of Josiah.

(3) The paragraph abruptly beginning in verse 6 dealing with the cutoff of Israel (Judah) and the scattering of the people is exilic. The exilic editor changes from a discussion of the dynasty of the house of David and the permanence of the temple, to the destruction and scattering of the people and the threat that the house will become

> . . . a heap of ruins (1 Kings 6:8).

Scholars have pointed out that the transitions of the Josianic historian from original source material tended to be smooth, but the transitions of the exilic editor were often abrupt.

Some scholars see in these words from Isaiah to Hezekiah a presumption of a failed dynasty:

> Days are coming when all that is in your house, and that which your ancestors have stored up until this day, shall be carried to Babylon; nothing shall be left, says the LORD. Some of your own sons who are born to you shall be taken away; they shall be eunuchs in the palace of the king of Babylon (2 Kings 20:17–18).

The Role of the People in the Exilic Edition

We have pointed out previously that one of the characteristics of the Josianic edition of DH was the tendency to tie the fate of the nation to the behavior of the monarch. In the exilic edition the people are made responsible. The phrase . . . *they would not listen* is a key exilic phrase. It is used to promote the role of prophetic warnings which went unheeded, further justifying the punishment of defeat and exile. For example:

"I sent to you . . . my servants the prophets." But *they would not listen* (2 Kings 17:14).

The phrase is also used to blame the people for ignoring the covenant between God and Israel.

". . . you shall not forget the covenant that I have made with you. You shall not fear other gods. . . ." However they would not listen (2 Kings 17:38–40).

Many scholars believe that the explanation of Israel's fall (the northern kingdom) following this verse in 2 Kings 17 is chiefly exilic:

In the ninth year of Hoshea, the King of Assyria captured Samaria, and he carried the Israelites away to Assyria, and placed them in Halah, and on the Habor, the river of Gozan, and in the city of the Medes (2 Kings 17:6).[4]

In the speech which follows the above verse (2 Kings 17:7–18) the exilic editor changed the viewpoint of the earlier Josianic edition which had blamed the fall of the north on the sins of Jeroboam, and placed the blame on *the people of Israel*. The main purpose for the exilic edition was to explain the fall of Judah, but in seeking that answer the editor had to rethink the reason given for the fall of Israel in the Josianic edition of DH. The kings of Israel had been blamed for the punishment of Israel (the northern kingdom) because they (the kings) walked in the sins of Jeroboam. When the blame is placed on the people (instead of the kings), this is a characteristic of the exilic editor. Notice in this verse that even the manufacture of the two golden calves was blamed on the people:

> And they forsook all the commandants of the LORD their God, and *made for themselves* molten images of two calves; and they made an Asherah and worshiped all the host of heaven, and served Baal (2 Kings 17:16).

Review

In the last two chapters we have looked at examples of the editorial additions to the Josianic edition of DH. In Joshua we noted that the conquest was changed from complete to incomplete. In Judges we suggested that the four part pattern (sin, punishment, repentance, deliverance) may have been superimposed on ancient deliverer stories to teach defeated, captive Israel that repentance was an option leading to deliverance. In Samuel we noted the attempt to harmonize both pro- and anti-monarchic traditions, and suggested that additional anti-monarchic traditions may have been introduced by the exilic editor. We also noted the use of the term *all Israel* in Samuel, a concept which was projected into Israel's ancient past by both the Josianic historian and the exilic editor. In Kings we pointed out exilic additions in such passages as this:

> . . . everyone passing by will say, "Why has the LORD done such a thing to this land and to this house?" (1 Kings 9:9).

Throughout all four scrolls (Joshua, Judges, Samuel, Kings) we noted exilic references to a covenant between Yahweh and *the people* of Israel. This was not the same as the covenant between Yahweh and the house of David which appeared in the Josianic edition of DH.

The exilic editor came to the conclusion that the complete fall of Israel (and Judah, see 1 Kings 17:19–20) was a sign of a punishment that was well deserved, that Yahweh had warned the people again and again by prophetic messengers, and that the scattered people of Yahweh had to admit their guilt, turn to Yahweh in repentance, and trust in his mercy to forgive them and restore them. In the ancient days of the judges, the people had turned from Yahweh and had experienced his wrath. When they cried out to him, however, he heard their cry and had delivered them from their enemies.

A Practice of the Exilic Editor

It is an assumption of this study that *the entire Josianic edition of DH* is now embedded in an exilic theological structure developed

---

CHART 9
CHARACTERISTICS OF THE EXILIC EDITION OF THE DEUTERONOMISTIC HISTORY

1. The exilic edition contained the entire Josianic edition. (See chart »5.)
2. The conquest of the land is incomplete, with Amorites (Canaanites) remaining in all areas.
3. The role of the people (in obeying or not obeying the law) is emphasized, and the role of the monarch is de-emphasized (after an early editorial expansion of the sins of Manasseh).
4. The Davidic promise is ignored.
5. A covenant is presented between Yahweh and the people based on *the vassal treaty form*.[6]
6. References to the scattering of the people and exile are present.
7. Further emphasis is placed on the *role of prophets* predicting the destruction of Israel and Judah.
8. The mercy of Yahweh is introduced and his willingness to hear the cry of the people wherever they are.
9. Further anti-monarchic material is introduced.
10. The phrase *they would not listen* is an exilic phrase used to indicate that the people were responsible for the destruction of Judah.

---

by the Deuteronomists or their heirs to explain the changed circumstances of Yahweh's people as a result of the destruction of Jerusalem and the temple. The editor (or editors) carefully and respectfully edited, enhanced and expanded the shorter, simpler version of DH, but they did not believe that it was their right or privilege to delete words, sentences or paragraphs from the scroll as they inherited it. This practice was a step in the development of the belief that certain inherited scrolls contained a sacred revelation from Yahweh. In the days of Josiah the Deuteronomists expanded the *oracles of Yahweh* as they had been delivered by four 8th century prophets, by placing the words of the prophets in a liturgical structure.[5] During the period of the exile, the Deuteronomists expanded the Josianic edition of DH by placing it in an expanded theological structure. The earlier edition forever took on the stamp of the perspective of a defeated nation in exile. In the chart on p. 86 we list the characteristics introduced by the exilic edition of DH.

If it were possible to read the Josianic edition of DH it would not be clear what role the people played in Israel's fate. Because of the art of the Deuteronomist however it is not possible to read the exilic edition of DH today without being convinced of their responsibility.

To clarify this, in the next chapter we will explain the difference between the covenant concept in the Josianic edition of DH and the exilic edition.

NOTES

1. It is ironic that this devastating passage, announcing the destruction of the temple, follows a passage where the LORD informs Solomon of the following promise:

> I have heard your prayer and your plea, which you made before me; I have consecrated this house that you have built, and put my name there forever; my eyes and my heart will be there for all time (1 Kings 9:3).

Why didn't the editor change this passage? We believe that it was the practice of the exilic editor not to omit words which were previously contained in the scroll he was editing. We will discuss this principle later in this book.

2. One of the sources of confusion involved in reading certain passages in DH and the 8th century prophets is the use of the name Israel. Israel sometimes means the northern kingdom only, as opposed to Judah, the southern kingdom. In this passage (1 Kings 9:7–9) it is obvious that Israel means Judah. Sometime after the destruction of Israel, 722 B.C.E., the name Israel began to be used for the people of Yahweh in Judah.

3. Deuteronomy 29 is identified as exilic by Nelson, A.D.H. Mayes, Weinfeld, and others. Parallels are pointed out between Deuteronomy and the book of Jeremiah also. We will discuss the structure of the book of Deuteronomy in chapter 10.

4. A. D. H. Mayes, in *Israel Between Settlement and Exile,* and other scholars, identify the speeches explaining the fall of Israel as a breaking of the covenant between Israel and Yahweh, as exilic. Exilic phrases such as *they would not listen* and *you shall not fear other gods* are cited. The identification of these passages, 2 Kings 17:7–20, and 2 Kings 17:34b–40 as exilic also depend on the identification of references to the Mosaic covenant between Yahweh and Israel, for which the law of Moses supplied the conditions, as exilic. This is the firm conclusion of Mayes in *Israel Between Settlement and Exile* (page 55 and others). Richard Elliot Friedman also takes this view in *The Exile and Biblical Narrative.* We will discuss the various meanings of the word covenant in our next chapter, "The Origin of Covenant Theology."

5. See our discussion of the 8th century prophets in chapter 11.

6. A.D.H. Mayes writes, "It was first he (the exilic editor) who introduced covenant thought and terminology" in *Israel Between Exile and Settlement*, page 50.

Chapter 9

THE ORIGIN OF COVENANT THEOLOGY

We do not know how large the Deuteronomistic circle was in the days of Josiah. It may have had few members. If this were the case their influence, ambition, and goals far exceeded their numerical strength. Around the monarchy of Josiah they intended to standardize and centralize the religious culture of Judah in preparation for the incorporation of the northern territories (their former home), an area which had been separated from Judah for centuries, devastated by the Assyrian war machine in the late 8th century (722). But Assyria was now in fatal decline, and a new age was on the horizon.

While we do not know the numerical strength or the precise social position of the Deuteronomists, we do know the following:

(1) They were the heirs of a Levitical priestly circle which had fled to Jerusalem from the Shechem/Shiloh area following the tragic events of 722.

(2) They brought with them northern traditions of Israel, including scrolls containing the original oracles of two 8th century prophets, Hosea and Amos, both of whom had been scathingly critical of the power structure of Samaria. They later added at least two more prophetic scrolls to their collection of sacred writings, Isaiah and Micah.

(3) The torah which they sponsored (the law collection which they later made the core of the book of Deuteronomy) was a vastly updated and enhanced version of an ancient law collection which became known as the Book of the Covenant (BC). This primitive law collection, inappropriately called *the book of the covenant,* was later inserted into the book of Exodus (20:22–23:19).

(4) Although they thought of themselves as preservers of an-

89

cient traditions, they were a powerfully creative and highly innova-
tive force in the development of the theology of ancient Judah.[1]

(5) They were zealous for Yahweh.

The Meaning of the Word Covenant

The word covenant is a theological word which has acquired a
tremendously heavy structure. As an author (raised in a covenant
theology tradition) I am acutely aware that even the exploration of
the meaning of this term can have a sleep-inducing effect on the
reader. For this reason I have decided to keep this necessary chapter
brief and simple. For those who find the going tough, a one sentence
summary of this chapter is provided at the end.

For a thousand years before the exile the Hebrew word for covenant had nothing whatever to do with the vassal treaty form. The
Hebrew word is built on three consonants, *BRT*, and means agreement, arrangement between two or several parties, a treaty, con-
tract, bargain, or obligation. It appears in English alliteration in
various forms: berit, berith, brith, and beyrith. The letters *BRT* form
the root of a noun.[2]

The word covenant is used to describe a great variety of relation-
ships. Here are three examples:

> I will make for you a covenant oh that day with the wild
> animals, the birds of the air, and the creeping things of the
> ground (Hosea 2:18).[3]

> They did not remember the covenant of kinship (Amos 1:9).

> We have made a covenant with death, and with Sheol we
> have an agreement (Isaiah 28:15).

How the Word Covenant Is Used in the
Josianic Edition of DH

In the Josianic edition of DH the word *berith* is used in a wide
variety of ways. Often the parties are identified. Here are three
examples:

> Jonathan made a covenant with David because he loved
> him (1 Samuel 18:3).

> ...and all the men of Jabesh said to Nahash, "Make a covenant (treaty) with us and we will serve you" (1 Samuel 11:1).

> But in the seventh year Jehoiada summoned the captains of the Carites and of the guards and had them come to him in the house of the LORD. He made a covenant with them and put them under an oath in the house of the LORD (2 Kings 11:4).

One meaning which the word *berith* did not have in the Josianic version was the structured meaning based on the *vassal treaty form*.

Covenant in the 8th Century Prophets

We have stated that the Levitical priests from the Shechem/Shiloh area brought with them (when they fled Israel) the scrolls of two prophets, Amos and Hosea. In Jerusalem they acquired the scrolls of two other 8th century prophets, Isaiah and Micah. In the original oracles of the four 8th century prophets, the concept of covenant, based on the vassal treaty form, did not appear. In the 8th century Yahweh was not conceived of as a covenant-loving God. In the book of Hosea, for example, the word *berith* appears five times. Only once can it be attributed to Hosea:

> ...they multiply falsehood and violence; they make a bargain (*berith*) with Assyria, and oil is carried to Egypt (Hosea 12:1).[4]

Notice that in this verse from Hosea, the *berith* is not between Yahweh and Israel, but between Samaria and Assyria. Likewise, there are no examples of the use of the word *berith* in the original oracles of Amos, Isaiah, or Micah. In order to understand how the idea of an ancient covenant based on an extended treaty form between Israel and Yahweh emerged, we have to review the Deuteronomists' fondness for the use of metaphor.

The Use of Metaphor by the Deuteronomists

In seeking to describe Israel, Israel's God, and the relationship between Israel and her God, the Deuteronomists of both the Josianic

period and the exile made generous use of metaphor. They had
learned the use of metaphor from the scroll of Hosea.

In the original oracles of Hosea, as identified by Gale Yee in her
dissertation *Composition and Tradition in the Book of Hosea, A Redactional Critical Investigation,*[5] 12 metaphors were used to describe
(the decision makers of) Israel. They were all negative. Before the
scroll of Hosea reached its final form it contained 27 metaphors for
Israel, nine added by the exilic editor of Hosea.[6] It also contained a
series of metaphors for Yahweh.

The Deuteronomists learned to use many metaphors to describe
the relationship between Israel and Yahweh. Three popular metaphors were parent and child (Hosea 11:1), husband and wife (Hosea
2:19), and protector and vassal (Isaiah 31:45). Following the devastation of Judah, when a profound and satisfactory answer to the question "Why had the LORD visited this severe punishment on his
people?" was desperately needed, the extended and complete development of the vassal treaty metaphor provided the answer. Before we
discuss the vassal treaty form (which provided the structure for
covenant theology) which in turn became the Bible's most extended
figure, we have to examine a common, repeated meaning of the
Hebrew word *berith* (covenant) in the Josianic edition of DH.

The Covenant with David

The covenant between Yahweh and David had nothing to do
with the vassal treaty form.[7] The vassal treaty form used in the 8th
century by Assyria[8] to subdue and compel the cooperation of small
near eastern nations like Israel and Judah contained restrictions,
conditions and stipulations. These conditions were recorded on a
scroll and deposited in the temple of the vassal. It was required that
this scroll be read publicly from time to time. God's promise to David, like his promise to Abraham of Hebron,[9] did not contain any
conditions. *It was unconditional.*

> Your house and your kingdom shall be made sure forever
> before me; your throne shall be established forever (2 Sam-
> uel 7:16).[10]

The promise made to David was unconditional. In an extensive
study of the subject by Moshe Weinfeld, *Deuteronomy and the
Deuteronomic School,*[11] the author demonstrates how the form of the

---

CHART 10
METAPHORS FOR ISRAEL USED BY HOSEA

2:2	Guilty Mother
2:4b	Harlot
5:13	A Sick Person
7:8	A Cake Not Turned
7:9	Gray Haired Man
7:11	A Silly Dove
8:8	A Useless Vessel
8:9	A Wild Ass
9:16	Dried Up Fruit Tree
10:11	Trained Heifer
12:7a	Dishonest Merchant
13:13	A Stubborn, Unborn Son

---

covenant with David, like the covenant with Abraham, was clearly differentiated from the *conditional* vassal treaty form.

The Josianic Historian Did Not Use the Vassal Treaty Form

For our purpose it is only necessary to understand that the form of covenant between David and Yahweh as it appears in the Josianic version of DH was based on a land grant form. In the land grant, a rich and powerful king selected an individual (in whom he found great pleasure) and his progeny for a gift of land. The recipient was rewarded for his faithfulness, to demonstrate the power and generosity of the king. No conditions were imposed. The descendants of the recipient were protected by the grant for perpetuity.

> But I will not take my steadfast love from him, as I took it from Saul, whom I put away from before you. Your house and your kingdom shall be made forever before me; your throne shall be established forever (2 Samuel 7:15–16).

The land grant was understood to be a gift for faithfulness:

> And Solomon said "You have shown great and steadfast love to your servant my father David, because he walked

CHART 11
EXCERPTS FROM THE VASSAL-TREATIES OF ESARHADDON*

The treaty (which) Esarhaddon, king of Assyria, has made with you, in the presence of the great gods of heaven and earth (lines 41–42).

You swear that you will not listen to, or conceal, any word which is evil, improper (or) unsuitable concerning Ashurpanipal, the crown prince . . . (108–109).

You swear that should anyone . . . speak to you of rebellion and insurrection . . . you will seize the perpetrators of insurrection . . . if you are able to put them to death you will put them to death, and you will destroy their name and their seed from the land . . . (130–141).

You swear that you, while serving this oath with your lips, will take responsibility for your sons which shall be after the treaty . . . your sons and your grandsons . . . (385–395).

You swear that you will not alter it (copy of treaty), you will not consign it to the fire nor throw it into the water, nor bury it in the earth nor destroy it by any cunning device . . . (410–413).

You swear that you will not loose yourselves from Esarhaddon . . . you will not go to the right or to the left. . . . May scorpions devour him who would go the the right, may scorpions devour him who would go to the left (632–636).

[The treaty text closes with more than 75 curses of various types.]

*THIS IS A TRANSLATION BY D. J. WISEMAN (LONDON: HARRISON AND SONS) 1958.

Moshe Weinfeld in the introduction to his Anchor Bible Commentary on Deuteronomy 1–11 stresses the *loyalty oath* nature of this treaty (Pages 6–9).

before you in faithfulness, in righteousness and in upright-
ness of heart toward you; and you have kept for him this
great and steadfast love" (1 Kings 3:6–7).[12]

An important element of the legal document describing the
grant was a statement of the boundaries of the land (for example
Genesis 15:18 and elsewhere).

The Problem Created by the Destruction
of Jerusalem and Judah

Following the tragic events of 587/6 the Josianic history became
outdated. What happened to the promise of Yahweh to the house of
David? Were the gods of the Babylonians (Chaldeans) greater than
Yahweh, the God of Israel? The exilic editor found his theological
answer in the structure of the vassal treaty form *which was conditional. The vassal treaty form became an extended metaphor.*

While Josiah was alive the promise to the House of David supported the Deuteronomic goal of centralization and standardization
and the exclusive worship of Yahweh. The exclusiveness of Yahweh
meant the elimination of every form of Canaanite and Assyrian
religious practice, as defined by the Deuteronomists. This meant
that the people of Judah had to be addressed for didactic purposes.
The role of the masses was recognized as a vital element in Judean
unity. It is possible that the torah which was read in public to the
people consisted of only the first several chapters (12–13) of the full
torah (Deuteronomy 12–26).[13]

This recognition of *the role of the people* in the Josianic version
of DH was a step in the direction of *the accountability of the people*
which played the vital role in the vassal treaty metaphor of the
exilic editor. His conclusion was that in addition to the promise to
David (called a covenant) there was another covenant based on the
vassal treaty form between Yahweh and the people of Israel. This
covenant would be spelled out in the exilic edition of the book of
Deuteronomy. It was reported to have been rehearsed on the plains
of Moab by Moses, according to the exilic editor, before the people
entered the land (pre-history) and Moses referred to its initiation as
taking place on the plains of Horeb ". . . with your fathers."

The exilic editor used this vassal treaty form of covenant to
explain the destruction of Jerusalem and the temple. The *people* had
not kept the conditions of this ancient covenant.

CHART 12
SECTIONS OF THE VASSAL POLITICAL TREATY FORM

1.	PREAMBLE	Identification of parties and statement of purpose of the relationship.
2.	HISTORICAL PROLOGUE	Antecedent history.
3.	BASIC STIPULATIONS	General principles.
4.	SPECIFIC STIPULATIONS AND CONDITIONS	Rules and regulations, statutes and ordinances.
5.	WITNESSES	Gods, and sometimes parts of nature, heaven and earth.
6.	BLESSINGS AND CURSES	Motivation for keeping treaty.
7.	OATH	Vassal swears to be faithful.
8.	DEPOSIT OF TREATY IN TEMPLE OF VASSAL	A scroll would contain a copy of the treaty principles and conditions.
9.	PROVISION FOR PERIODIC READING OF THE TREATY	The scroll would be read in public to remind officials and people of the conditions and purposes of the treaty.

Two (or more) different uses of the word covenant in the canonical version of the books of Joshua, Judges, Samuel and Kings confuse the modern reader. But notice that nowhere in the final version of DH does the editor explain the elements of the vassal treaty. So the good news is that we only have to remember two things: (1) in the vassal treaty formula the people constituted a party, and (2) the vassal treaty form of covenant was conditional.

It is only if we wish to understand the structure of the exilic edition of the book of Deuteronomy that we have to become familiar with the elements of the Assyrian vassal treaty form. We turn to the book of Deuteronomy in our next chapter.

One Sentence Summary

The covenant based on the ancient near eastern vassal treaty form was a reinterpretation of Israel's history *by the exilic heirs* of the Deuteronomic circle of the days of Josiah to explain the ultimate destruction of Jerusalem and the temple of Yahweh in 586 B.C.E.

NOTES

1. Saul Olyan in his book *Asherah and the Cult of Yahweh in Israel* (Atlanta: Scholars Press, 1988), writes: "The Deuteronomistic school are evidently the innovators, though in their polemic they claim that their position is traditional and ancient" (page 9).

2. There are a few scattered examples of the use of the word covenant as a verb in some English translations. In the KJV in 2 Chronicles 7:18 it says, "I covenanted with your father David," but in the NRSV it says, "I made a covenant with your father David."

3. This is the translation of the NRSV.

4. This is the translation of the RSV. In the NRSV the verse reads as follows: ". . . they multiply falsehood and violence; they make a treaty with Assyria, and oil is carried to Egypt."

5. Gale Yee, *Composition and Tradition in the Book of Hosea, A Redactional Critical Investigation* (New York: Scholars Press, 1987).

6. The exilic editor of Hosea was the same editor (or at least a member of the same circle of scribes) who edited and produced the exilic version of DH.

7. The ancient Hittite vassal treaty form minimally had these six elements: (1) a preamble identifying the powerful monarch, the suzerain, (2) historical information identifying the beneficial acts of the suzerain on behalf of the vassal, (3) conditions and stipulations, including one that stated and restated the need to remain faithful to the powerful party and not seek alliances with other foreign powers, (4) requirement that the written document containing the stipulations be placed in the temple of the vassal and read in public from time to time, (5) a list of witnesses, sometimes gods and sometimes deified parts of nature like heaven and earth, and (6) curses and blessings. See E.W. Nicholson, *God and His People, Covenant and Theology in the Old Testament* (Oxford: Clarendon Press, 1986), pages 57–58.

8. We have copies of ancient vassal treaties used by the Assyrians. Many of the elements of a vassal treaty of the Assyrian king Esarhaddon have found their way into the book of Deuteronomy as we will point out in our next chapter.

9. It is interesting that Hebron was the home of Abraham (Genesis 13:18) and also David's first capital of Judah (2 Samuel 2:1). It seems as if Hebron was the home of the unconditional covenant.

10. Read the entire 7th chapter of 2 Samuel.

11. Moshe Weinfeld, *Deuteronomy and the Deuteronomic School* (Oxford: University Press, 1983), pages 74–82.

12. To David the promise was dynasty. For Abraham the promise was progeny. Both are combined by the P author in Genesis by these words about Sarah: "I will bless her, and she shall give rise to nations; kings of people shall come from her" (Genesis 17:16).

13. It is possible that the book of the law found in the temple and read to Josiah, and by Josiah, consisted of only the first several chapters (Deuteronomy 12–13) which dealt exclusively with cultic purity. The torah was said to be read twice in one day (1 Kings 22:8–10). The remaining chapters, 14–26, may have been incorporated at a later time.

Chapter 10

THE BOOK OF DEUTERONOMY

The Moses we encounter in the book of Deuteronomy is not the same Moses found in the book of Exodus. We will note three examples.

(a) In Exodus, when Moses was instructed by God to address the Hebrews he replied:

> O my Lord, I have never been eloquent, neither in the past nor even now that you have spoken to your servant; but I am slow of speech and slow of tongue (Exodus 4:10).

God agrees with Moses and promises him help:

> . . . he (Aaron) shall speak for you to the people; he shall serve as a mouth for you, and you shall serve as God for him (Exodus 4:16).

In a doublet of the above call, the same tradition is repeated:

> But Moses spoke to the LORD, "The Israelites have not listened to me; how then shall Pharaoh listen to me, poor speaker that I am" (Exodus 6:12).

Unlike the Moses of Exodus however, the Moses of Deuteronomy needs no one to speak for him.[1] This Moses is history's greatest orator and the teacher of the law *par excellence*. In Deuteronomy Moses is able to recall detailed incidents of the past, summarize decades and periods of former activity, and draw powerful and relevant theological conclusions from both with clarity and driving force.

In many ways the Moses of Deuteronomy differs from the Moses of other traditions. The Moses of the tetrateuch (Exodus to Numbers) was a multi-faceted person, a man of action, a labor organizer, a miracle worker, a judge, a warrior, a negotiator, and the player of a dozen other roles.[2] In Deuteronomy Moses is the elder statesman who delivers the world's greatest farewell address.

(b) Another difference to note about Moses in Deuteronomy is that he is not linked with Aaron. In the previous four books, Aaron is repeatedly referred to as the brother of Moses.[3] In Deuteronomy, the only time Aaron is mentioned is when Moses speaks critically about him, and to report that Aaron died.[4] Moses does not identify Aaron as his brother:

> The LORD was so angry with Aaron that he was ready to destroy him, but I interceded also on behalf of Aaron at that same time (Deuteronomy 9:20).

(c) The Moses of Deuteronomy is also a cabinet maker.[5] He makes the ark of the covenant:

> So I made an ark of acacia wood. . . . I turned and came down the mountain, and put the tablets in the ark that I had made (Deuteronomy 10:3–5).

The ark which Moses makes in Deuteronomy is only a chest, not the elaborate ark described in Exodus 25:10–22, which is overlaid with gold, has four rings of gold, poles covered with gold, and two golden cherubim (of hammered work) with wings which overshadow something called the mercy seat. In Exodus Moses is instructed to have the Israelites make this elaborate ark. The Exodus account is clearly from a different tradition.

The Core of the Book of Deuteronomy

There are four collections of law in the Hebrew Bible. All are found in the first five books:

(1) The Book of the Covenant (Exodus 20:22–23:33).
(2) Holiness Code (Leviticus 17–26).
(3) The Priestly Code (scattered throughout the tetrateuch).
(4) The Deuteronomic Torah (Deuteronomy 12–26).

The book of Deuteronomy is the only book of the Hebrew Bible which has as its core a collection of laws. Deuteronomy grew from the center out, with several introductions added and a number of sections added following the core.[6]

The growth of the Deuteronomic torah (*sepher hatorah*) is a lifelong study in itself. Gerhard von Rad's words concerning both the torah and the whole canonical book of Deuteronomy best summarize the growth of the book for us: "Deuteronomy must have had an unusually complicated previous history. . . . Deuteronomy presents itself to us almost as a mosaic of innumerable, extremely varied pieces of traditional material. But at the same time this is not to deny that the book must nevertheless in the last resort be understood as a unity."

What Is Our Purpose in This Chapter?

In this book we are assuming that the Josianic edition of the Deuteronomistic history (Joshua, Judges, Samuel, Kings) appeared before the first destruction of Jerusalem (597/6) with a shortened form of the book of Deuteronomy as an introduction or prologue. Chapter 22 of Kings informs us of the discovery of the book of the law in the temple and the reading of the book of the law to King Josiah. Later Josiah read the book to the people.

> The king went up to the house of the LORD, and with him went all the people of Judah . . . both small and great; he read in their hearing all the words of the book of the covenant that had been found in the house of the LORD (2 Kings 23:2).

It would be easy for us if we could assume that the book of the law which Josiah read to the people now appears in chapters 12–26 of Deuteronomy and that the Josianic edition of Deuteronomy consisted of this law collection prefaced by narrative material beginning with Deuteronomy 4:44:[7]

> This is the law which Moses set before the Israelites.

Unfortunately our task is not that easy. First notice that in the verse which states that Josiah read the book to the people the name of the book has been changed. It is not called the book of the law, but the *book of the covenant* (2 Kings 23:2). In an earlier chapter we suggested that the account of Josiah's activities is more complex than it first appears. (See in our chapter 4, the section entitled Who Was Josiah?)

So our problem is twofold. First, the account of Josiah in Kings may have several levels of authorship, one level produced before the destruction of Jerusalem, and another developed during the exile. Second, we don't know for sure what the contents of the book read by Josiah to the people consisted of. In other words we cannot assume that the book of the law found in the temple was the identical collection now found in chapters 12 through 26 of the canonical book of Deuteronomy. As a matter of fact we can almost be assured that the book of the law grew during the exile with some additions.

What Book Did Josiah Read?

We are assuming the historicity of Josiah, the appearance of *a* book of laws during his reign, and a public reading from a book of laws by Josiah.[8] This would be consistent with the didactic purpose of the Deuteronomists, and in harmony with the goal of national unity and centralization of worship in accordance with Deuteronomic principles. Since we are sure that the core of the Josianic edition consisted of ". . . the book of the law" it would be good if we could include chapters 12–26 as being part of the Josianic edition of DH. But we don't know for sure which words King Josiah read to the people. It is hard to imagine Josiah reading the entire torah (collection of laws) which included laws governing diet, witnesses, female captives, rebellious children, your neighbor's donkey or ox, sexual relations, marriage and divorce, weights, murder, interest on loans, and boiling a kid in its mother's milk. It is easier to imagine Josiah reading *the opening chapters* of the torah however (chapters 12–13) which deal with cultic purity and the establishment of a central shrine, and this shorter reading would have more impact on the listeners and better serve the Deuteronomic purpose of centralizing and standardizing the cult of Yahweh in Jerusalem:

> But you shall seek the place that the LORD your God will choose out of all your tribes as his habitation to put his name there. You shall go there, bringing your burnt offerings and your sacrifices, your tithes and your donations, your votive gifts, your freewill offerings, and the firstlings

of your herds and flocks. And you shall eat there in the presence of the LORD your God, you and your households together, rejoicing in all the undertakings in which the LORD your God has blessed you (Deuteronomy 12:5–7).

Since there is no assurance as to what the book contained which Josiah read, we can only speculate. Our speculation is that Josiah did not read all the words of the Deuteronomic (or Deuteronomistic) torah, but that it is possible that more than the laws of cultic purity appeared in the Josianic edition of Deuteronomy. It is almost certain that some portions of the torah (12–26) were added during the exile however, and even later.[9]

The Josianic Edition of Deuteronomy

We can begin our determination by a process of elimination. The first three chapters of Deuteronomy were added much later to connect Deuteronomy with the tetrateuch. There is general agreement that material in the rear of the book was not part of the earlier versions. This would include the Song of Moses (chapters 31:30–32:44), the Blessings of Moses (chapter 33:1–29), and the account of the death of Moses (chapter 34:1–12).

Basically this would leave chapters 4 through 30 for further consideration.[10] Most scholars agree that the break between chapter 3 and chapter 4 is complete.[11] Chapter 4 starts with a sermon which has exilic themes, obedience to the law and the prohibition of images. This exhortatory sermon continues through verse 40. Verses 41 through 43 establish cities of refuge, east of the Jordan. (These verses may have been added to Deuteronomy when it became attached to the tetrateuch, after the captivity.)

So there are two possible starting points for the Josianic edition of Deuteronomy. One is 4:44:

This is the law which Moses set before the Israelites,

Another possible opening is supplied in 5:1:

Moses convened all Israel, and said to them: Hear, O Israel, the statutes and ordinances that I am addressing to you today; you shall learn them and observe them diligently.

Notice that in each possible opening, Moses is spoken of in *the third person*, indicating not a speech of Moses but the hand of an editor.[12]

We believe that the Josianic edition of Deuteronomy consisted of an historical, hortatory introduction[13] which tied Moses to the torah which follows, and some concluding material. The concluding material may have consisted of a portion of chapter 28, verses 3–6 (rudimentary blessings) and 16–19 (rudimentary curses), a closing liturgy for the reading of the law, a liturgy which was originally used at the time of offering of first fruits.[14] Like all other portions of the Josianic edition of DH, Deuteronomy (the prologue) had to be overhauled after the humiliation of Judah, the destruction of Jerusalem and the temple of Yahweh.

The Exilic Edition of Deuteronomy

To enhance our understanding of the exilic edition of the book of Deuteronomy we have to define some of our terms. We do this with the use of a short list.

(a) The exilic edition of Deuteronomy was produced by the heirs of the Deuteronomic circle of Jerusalem sometime after the destruction of Jerusalem. This circle was possibly located in Egypt.

(b) The exilic edition of Deuteronomy contained all the material of the Josianic edition strategically expanded.

(c) While there is a difference between the exilic edition and the canonical (final) edition of Deuteronomy, the exilic edition contained all or most of the essential sections of the final form of the book.

(d) Although the book of Deuteronomy does not *present itself* as a theological form of the political vassal treaty, it is obvious that the exilic form of Deuteronomy was influenced by the vassal treaty at three levels: form, vocabulary, and imagery.

Form of the Vassal Treaty

The exilic editor in particular, and the heirs of the Deuteronomic circle in general, found the answer to the question *Why was Judah defeated and destroyed by the Chaldeans?* The form of a ceremony establishing a near eastern political treaty relationship (the vassal relationship) provided the answer and presented the editor with a new interpretation of Israel's past and her relationship with her God, Yahweh.

```
CHART 13
SECTIONS OF THE VASSAL TREATY
IN DEUTERONOMY
```

1.	PREAMBLE	Chapter 5:6.
2.	HISTORICAL PROLOGUE	Chapter 1:6 to 5:6.
3.	BASIC STIPULA-TIONS	Chapter 4:1–23; 6:4–7; 26:10–22.
4.	SPECIFIC STIPU-LATIONS AND CONDITIONS	Chapters 12–26.
5.	WITNESSES	Chapters 4:26; 30:19; 31:28.
6.	BLESSINGS AND CURSES	Chapters 27 and 28.
7.	OATH	Chapter 29:9–28.
8.	DEPOSIT OF TREATY IN TEMPLE OF VASSAL	Chapters 10:1–5; 31:24–26.
9.	PROVISION FOR PERIODIC READ-ING OF THE TREATY	Chapter 31:9–16.

In Israel's ancient past, says this interpretation, Israel was a small, weak nation in need of a strong protective power. Even before entering the land this protective power was found in Yahweh, a champion of the weak and dispossessed, the God of the Hebrews, a people who gave meaning to the term *marginal*. This relationship between Yahweh and Israel was conceived of as having the chief elements of the near eastern vassal treaty form. The partners were Yahweh and Israel. Like all vassal treaty agreements, the relationship was conditional, and the conditions were spelled out in the Deuteronomic torah and summarized in the ten commandments (Deuteronomy 5:6–21). Yahweh had not saved Jerusalem and the temple from destruction because his people had repeatedly failed to observe the conditions of the *ancient* vassal-like relationship.

Influence on the Deuteronomists of the Political Treaty Ceremony

We find the most relevant form (for our purposes) of the vassal treaty to be the form used by the Assyrian king Esarhaddon (681–669). The vassal treaty arrangement was a very ancient and practical tool for great, powerful states with imperialistic goals to control smaller, weaker states. While statements in the treaty would idealistically stress the advantage of the arrangement for both parties (we will discuss the imagery of the treaty below) the chief advantage was to the powerful state which wanted to create a grateful ally in the small state, in addition to creating a source of tribute and natural resources to strengthen the suzerain and to improve the quality of life for the greater power, consistent with the imperialistic goals of the superpower.

An impressive ceremony initiated the vassal relationship in the capital city of the vassal, next to the temple of the vassal. When biblical scholars refer to the sections of the vassal treaty they are sometimes referring to the treaty itself and other times referring to the public ceremony to establish or renew the relationship.

The main sections of the vassal treaty form are found in the exilic form of the book of Deuteronomy (See chart #12.) The Deuteronomistic circle was no doubt familiar with the parts of the ceremony to establish (or renew) the vassal treaty relationship between Judah and Assyria.[15]

Influenced by the 8th century prophets, especially Hosea and Isaiah who vehemently opposed foreign alliances, it is not surprising that the exilic heirs of the Deuteronomic circle (the Deuteronomists) saw the religious imagery and the liturgical possibilities of the political treaty ceremony.

The exilic Deuteronomistic circle produced a magnificent liturgical script to serve as a prologue to the reading of their history (DH). The world would later call the script Deuteronomy.[16]

The Josianic edition of Deuteronomy (written before the destruction of Jerusalem) had a different purpose than the exilic edition. The Josianic edition of Deuteronomy had served as a literary tool to promote the optimistic spirit of nationalism in Judah and the centralization and standardization of Yahwism in Jerusalem. For this reason the Josianic edition had addressed the people of Judah/Israel for didactic purposes. In the exilic edition the people of Israel were addressed as one of the parties in the political treaty agreement, as the vassal, because it made no sense to address the monarchy which had been virtually destroyed. This view of the people of Israel as a party accountable to Yahweh had its roots among the Levitical priesthood of Shechem as far back as the time of the united monarchy of David and Solomon, and is preserved for us in the tradition which has the son of Solomon traveling to Shechem to negotiate with the people of Israel to be recognized as king. We will be reviewing this viewpoint in our chapter 13, "Going Back to the Beginning," and chapter 14, "Justice Themes and the Deuteronomists."

In recounting the establishment of the *ancient covenant* the exilic editor made it clear that the people were responsible for breaking the covenant, and the blame was not placed solely on the kings such as Jeroboam and Manasseh.

> . . . you once stood before the LORD your God at Horeb, when the LORD said to me, "Assemble *the people* for me, and I will let them hear my words, so that they may learn to fear me as long as they live on the earth, and may teach their children so. . . . He declared to you his covenant (*berith*) which he charged you to observe (Deuteronomy 4:10).

Then Moses informs the people what will happen to them if they do not keep the covenant.

> The LORD will scatter you among the people; only a few of you will be left among the nations where the LORD will lead you (Deuteronomy 4:27).

At the time the above words were penned Israel had been scattered into Assyria and elsewhere, and Judah had been scattered to Babylon and Egypt. Only the poor of the land remained in Judah.

Summary: The Growth of the Book of Deuteronomy[17]

There is no agreement among scholars concerning the precise steps involved in the growth of the book of Deuteronomy. Below is a possible outline.

(1) Deuteronomy first emerged during the reign of Josiah as a document for public reading by a Deuteronomic scribe or priest. It had a didactic purpose. It was read in the temple to support Josiah's program of political expansion and the Deuteronomic goal of centralization and standardization of the worship of Yahweh. The opening verse was 6:4:[18]

Hear (*shema*) O Israel: The LORD is our God, the LORD alone.

The powerful message of the entire document was that there was one God for one people, and one place to worship the one God. It was the place which the LORD thy God (*Yahweh thy God*) had chosen for his name to dwell. The name theology was characteristic of the pre-exilic Deuteronomic circle.

Not all the material now located from 6:4 through chapter 11 was found in the earliest edition. The section from 9:9 to 10:11 is written in the first person and was added in the second stage of the scroll's development.

There was no indication in the first stage that Moses was the speaker. This early edition of Deuteronomy started with a short historical prelude which prepared the listeners for the reading of the torah, the statutes and ordinances.[19] During the short historical review, at least six times past blessings to Israel were stated to be in accordance with a promise (*berith*) from Yahweh to Israel's ancestors (6:10; 7:8; 7:12; 8:1; 8:18; 9:5). Later an editor will add the names "Abraham, Isaac, and Jacob" after the word ancestors. The promise to Israel's ancestors was the basis for the establishment of a binding and powerful relationship between an idealized united Israel and Yahweh. This relationship did not have the characteristics of the vassal treaty form at this stage. Not only was there no mention of Moses in this early document, there also was no mention of the plains of Moab.

The torah, which was read after the historical prelude, was shorter than the torah of the canonical edition. There is no doubt however that the law of the central sanctuary was included (12:1–27). Also included was the section now located in 26:1–15 which includes the ancient creed beginning with the words:

A wandering Aramean was my ancestor . . . (26:5).

Following the reading of the collection of laws a concluding benediction borrowed from the feast of first fruits, was pronounced containing rudimentary blessings and curses (28:1–6 and 15–19).[20]

(2) After the Deuteronomic circle produced the Josianic history of Israel, which scholars now refer to as DH (the work of DTR 1, Joshua, Judges, Samuel, Kings), a decision was made to enlarge the early document discussed in paragraph (1) above and allow the expanded scroll to serve as an introduction to the written history. It was at this time that Moses was introduced as the speaker. A new beginning was added at 4:44.[21]

This is the law which Moses set before the Israelites.

The purpose of introducing Moses into the scroll of Deuteronomy was at least twofold. (a) Moses became the prototype of Joshua and Josiah, a perfect and obedient servant of Yahweh, and (b) Moses became the person who would receive the details of the lengthy torah which he would preserve and read to the people. The Shechemite tradition of Horeb was included. At Horeb, which may not have been a mountain in the Shechemite tradition, the ten commandments were said to be heard by all the people. The long detailed laws of the torah (beginning in chapter 12) would be given to Moses (instead of the people) by Yahweh, because of the fear of the people. They say to Moses:

Go near, you yourself, and hear all that the LORD our God tells you, and we will listen and do it (Deuteronomy 5:27).

A section of first person material (Moses is the speaker), Deuteronomy 9:9–10:11, was inserted into the earlier introduction (see paragraph 1), beginning with these words:

When I went up the mountain to receive the stone tablets . . . I remained on the mountain forty days and forty nights (9:9).

In this section (9:9 to 10:11) it is interesting to note that the expression "forty days and forty nights" appears five times. The numbers five and forty were both favorites of the Deuteronomic circle.

CHART 14
**THE GROWTH OF THE BOOK OF DEUTERONOMY IN
FIVE MAJOR STAGES**

1. In its earliest form Deuteronomy was an independent
    scroll with no connection to DH. Moses was not
    mentioned.

Original Intro. 6:4–11:31*	Short Torah 12–13 (?)	Rudimentary Bless-ings and curses 28:1–6, 15–19

2. All three sections were expanded (intro., torah, blessings) to
    serve as an prelude to the Josianic version of DH. *Moses was
    introduced at this stage.*

Second Intro. 4:44ff.	Original Intro. 6:4–11:31	Torah 12–13+	Expanded Blessings Chapter 27:1–9; 28:7–14

3. Deuteronomy continued to grow from the middle out. The
    exilic version of Deuteronomy consisted of all sections noted
    in the above paragraph (2) but was *bracketed* by a profound
    theological statement based on the metaphor of the near
    eastern vassal, political treaty (4:1–40 and chapters 29–30).
    The torah was greatly expanded to include additional civil
    laws from various sources. Collections of curses were also
    expanded.

Opening Statement 4:1–40	Second Intro. 4:44ff.	Original Intro. 6:4–11:31	Torah 12–26:15	Expanded Curses 27–28	Closing Statement 29–30

4. Following the exile, the book was further bracketed by chapters 1–3 and 33:1–10. This added *framework* reached back to Horeb (1:6) tying Deuteronomy to the tetrateuch, and forward to Joshua 3:28 and 31:7), making the enlarged book a bridge between the tetrateuch and the exilic version of DH.

| Post-Exilic Introduction 1–3 | (SEE BOX 3 ABOVE) 4:1 to 30:20 | Post-Exilic Conclusion 31:1–10 |

---

5. Sometime after the exile, editors added the closing chapters of Deuteronomy from various sources, Song of Moses (32), Blessing of Moses (33), Death of Moses (34).

*Excluding some paragraphs added later, for example, first person account from 9:9 to 10:11. See text.

In accordance with the Josianic version of DH, the complete conquest of the land was implied:

Know then today that the LORD your God is the one who crosses over before you as a devouring fire; he will defeat them (the Amorites) and subdue them before you, so that you may dispossess and destroy them quickly, as the LORD has promised you (Deuteronomy 9:3).

. . . the LORD is dispossessing them (Deuteronomy 9:4).

The body of legal material, the torah, was extended during this stage. The statutes and ordinances (now found in chapters 12 to 26:15) were not considered as conditions of a covenant since this second stage version of Deuteronomy still had no vassal treaty characteristics.

In accordance with the optimistic viewpoint of the Josianic version of DH, the blessings following the torah were enlarged. The paragraph now found following 28:7 was added, beginning with the words:

The LORD will cause your enemies who rise against you to
be defeated before you; they shall come out against you one
way, and flee before you seven ways (28:7).

The untimely death of Josiah, followed by the rapid decline and
fall of Judah as an independent political entity, ended an optimistic
period for the Deuteronomic circle. The subsequent destruction of
Judah and Jerusalem created the need for a revised and enlarged
version of DH. Deuteronomy would be further enlarged to become a
powerful introduction to a new understanding of Israel's history.

(3) Following decades of exile, the heirs of the Deuteronomic
circle, the Deuteronomists, developed a new understanding of Israel's previous relationship to her God. This new understanding was
an extended metaphor based on the near eastern political form
known to us as the vassal treaty (See Chapter 9, The Origin of
Covenant Theology).

The entire written history, DH, was updated in accordance with
this new understanding, as was the book of Deuteronomy.

The opening chapters of the canonical book of Deuteronomy can
be understood as written under the influence of the vassal political
treaty and presuppose a scattered, exilic community. This is illustrated for us in a profound theological statement which appears in
two parts (chapter 4:1–40 and chapters 29–30) This two-section theological statement was added at the beginning and end of the Deuteronomy scroll. This practice is referred to as bracketing. Bracketing
was a common practice of the Deuteronomistic scribes.

In the heart of chapter 4 we read this exilic statement:

The LORD will scatter you among the peoples . . . from
there you will seek the LORD your God, and you will find
him if you search for him with all your heart and soul. In
your distress when all these things have happened to you in
time to come, you will return to the LORD your God and
heed him. Because the LORD your God is a merciful God,
he will neither abandon you nor destroy you (Deuteronomy
4:27–31).

One of the ironies of the theology of ancient Israel is that it was as a
result of the destruction of Judah and the scattering of the people
that the concepts of Yahweh's universality and Yahweh's mercy
emerged so powerfully. The exilic introduction to the growing book

of Deuteronomy, like Second Isaiah, declared not only the futility of images and idols, but the uniqueness of Israel and Israel's God.

Chapters 29 and 30 are a continuation of chapter 4. The same exilic audience is assumed as the hearer or reader.

> . . . so the anger of the LORD was kindled against that land (foreigners will say). . . . The LORD uprooted them from their land in anger, fury, and great wrath, and cast them into another land, as is now the case (Deuteronomy 29:27–28).

The "curses" section was also greatly enlarged late in the exile. In the earliest form of Deuteronomy the "blessings and curses" served as the benediction for a law code liturgy. Later, during the exile, under the influence of the vassal treaty metaphor, many additional curses were added. This would include 27:11–26 and 28:15–44. These words were part of the exilic expansion:

> The LORD will bring you, and the king whom you set over you, to a nation that neither you nor your ancestors have known (28:36).

> The LORD will bring a nation from far away, from the end of the earth, to swoop down on you like an eagle, a nation whose language you do not understand (28:49).

It is pointed out by scholars that the Assyrian vassal treaty form of the 8th century did not have blessings, only curses, but that an ancient Hittite form of the vassal treaty did contain blessings. I do not believe that the Deuteronomists were influenced by the older Hittite treaty form, which was in use before the emergence of Israel in the thirteenth century. The scribes of the Deuteronomic circle may not have been aware of its existence. I believe the blessings, which are not as numerous as the curses, were included because of the influence of the Shechemite tradition of blessings and curses involving an ancient ritual near Mount Gerizim and Mount Ebal (Deuteronomy 11:29–30 and Joshua 8:33–34) and the use of the priestly benediction to close the earliest version of Deuteronomy (paragraph 1) borrowed from the ritual of the presentation of first fruits. Notice that the earliest blessings and curses (28:3–6, 15–19) were agricultural.

(4) Following the exile, with the emergence of the tetrateuch (Genesis, Exodus, Leviticus, Numbers), the scroll of Deuteronomy

was further bracketed by the addition of chapters 1–3 and 33:1–10. This added *framework* (another example of bracketing) reached further back in detail to Horeb (1:6) and the wilderness wanderings, tying Deuteronomy to the tetrateuch, and forward to Joshua (Joshua 3:28 and 31:7), making the enlarged book a bridge between the tetrateuch and the exilic version of DH.

(5) As a cohesive self-conscious group, the Deuteronomistic circle did not survive into the post-exilic period. In the area of Jerusalem the returning Babylonian Judahite community struggled with Judahites who had never been exiled to Babylon for control of religion in the newly established Persian province.

Years after the destruction of Babylon, during the restoration, at the time of the activity of Nehemiah and Ezra, there was a period of renewed scribal activity producing a new history of Israel (Chronicles). At this time the closing chapters of Deuteronomy were added to the inherited book from various sources, the Song of Moses (32), Blessing of Moses (33), and the Death of Moses (34).

NOTES

1.   It is only in the two call traditions that the weakness of Moses as a speaker is referred to. After the call, Moses does all his own speaking without any assistance from Aaron. There is a little puzzle here. Could this "weakness of speech" tradition have been promoted by the Aaronid priesthood of the Josianic period to promote the role played by Aaron in ancient Egypt? This is only speculation however.

2.   By our definition Moses is pre-historical, having never set foot in the land of Canaan. This makes Moses an institution, an excellent object of study for the student who would desire to become familiar with the many factions existent in ancient Israelite society. Obviously, there were differing Mosaic traditions in different locations and different periods of Israel's history. An attempt to merge these traditions is made in the books of Exodus to Numbers. There, as in the book of Deuteronomy, we can learn much about the values of the differing authors and scribal circles which produced the scrolls.

3.   Aaron is specifically referred to as the brother of Moses in Exodus 4:14; 7:1; 7:2; 28:1; 28:2; Leviticus 16:2; Numbers 20:8;

27:13. The Aaronid priests who put together the tetrateuch, after the Deuteronomistic history made its appearance, needed to establish that their traditional founder, Aaron, was recognized as the brother of Moses.

4. There is one mention of Aaron as the brother of Moses in Deuteronomy. It is a very late addition to the book of Deuteronomy and is copied from Numbers, chapter 20.

5. Moses is also a stone cutter. He says, "So I cut two tablets of stone like the former ones" (Deuteronomy 10:3).

6. Many of the books of the Hebrew Bible have a history of growth involving added beginnings and endings. This is obviously true of Amos and Hosea. The book of Judges has an added beginning (Chapter 1:1–2:5). 2 Kings has an added ending. There are other examples of added beginnings and endings. The first section of Isaiah has an added narrative ending (Isaiah 36–39).

7. Gerhard von Rad in his commentary on *Deuteronomy* (Philadelphia: Westminster, 1975), page 12, states that Deuteronomy 4:44 to 30:20 forms a complete book in itself.

8. Some scholars do not believe that Josiah read from a book of laws to the people. See for example A.D.H. Mayes in his commentary on *Deuteronomy* (Grand Rapids: Eerdmans, 1979), pages 98–103.

9. For example, A.D.H. Mayes in his commentary on *Deuteronomy* states that chapter 26 and the final part of chapter 25 are definitely exilic. See pages 330–340 and page 348.

10. A late passage between the Song of Moses and the Blessings of Moses (chapter 34:48–52) is attributed to the priestly source (P). See NJBC, page 108.

11. For example, von Rad, *Deuteronomy*, page 48, and Mayes, *Deuteronomy*, page 148.

12. There is little agreement concerning the first verse of the original book of Deuteronomy. E. W. Nicholson in his book *God and*

His People (Oxford: Clarendon, 1986), page 112, says that the opening verse of the original book of Deuteronomy was probably 6:4:

Hear, O Israel: The LORD is our God, the LORD alone.

13.   E. W. Nicholson in his book *God and His People, Covenant and Theology in the Old Testament* (Oxford: Clarendon Press, 1986), states that the earliest form of Deuteronomy started with 6:4, "Hear, O Israel: The Lord is our God, the LORD alone." See page 122ff.

14.   See A.D.H. Mayes, *Deuteronomy*, pages 348–358 for a thorough discussion of the growth of chapter 28.

15.   There are two treaty forms referred to by scholars, the Hittite form (2nd millennium) and the Assyrian form (1st millennium). It is beyond the scope of this book to deal with the differences. The treaty form most frequently cited is described by Moshe Weinfeld in his book *Deuteronomy and the Deuteronomic School*, pages 59–146. It is the treaty of the Assyrian king Esarhaddon (681–669 B.C.E.), predecessor of Ashurbanipal. The student is also referred to a description of the ancient vassal treaty and its relationship to Deuteronomy in a book by Peter Craigie, *Deuteronomy* (Grand Rapids: Eerdmans, 1976), pages 20–32. While Craigie's book takes a very conservative approach, the explanation of the vassal treaty form is valuable for its clarity.

16.   The Jewish name for Deuteronomy is *These Are The Words (Debarim)*, based on the opening words of the canonical book of Deuteronomy.

17.   For an excellent concise statement concerning the possible development of the book of Deuteronomy the student is referred to the article on Deuteronomy (both the introduction and the commentary) by Joseph Blenkinsopp in *NJBC*, pages 94–109.

18.   See E. W. Nicholson, *God and His People*, page 112.

19.   One of the problems which a student of the canonical book of Deuteronomy has to deal with is the difficulty of distinguishing between the voices of several speakers. There are at least three voices, (a) the Deuteronomic narrator, (b) Moses, and (c) Yahweh, and the speaker changes without notification to the reader. There

are places where the narrator tells the reader what Moses says that God said. It is beyond the scope of this book to deal extensively with the voices. The extent of this problem is elaborately discussed in a book by Robert Polzin, *Moses and the Deuteronomic History*.

20. Weinfeld in his commentary *Deuteronomy 1–11* ties the blessings and curses following the reading of the law to an ancient Shechem tradition, pages 11–13. Hays in *Deuteronomy*, page 351, states that blessings and curses were associated with law codes from ancient times.

21. See Gerhard von Rad, *Deuteronomy*, page 12, and Weinfeld, *Deuteronomy 1–11*, pages 9–10.

Chapter 11

THE EIGHTH CENTURY PROPHETS

Review

During the reign of Josiah (640–609), a period of great national-istic optimism for Judah, a small circle of Levitical priests who were zealous for Yahweh produced a theological history of Israel/Judah for public reading (DH). The first edition of this history (the Josianic edition) was shorter than the canonical version (Joshua, Judges, Samuel and Kings) which appears in our Bible.

This circle also produced a liturgical prologue and epilogue for the history. The prologue grew into the book of Deuteronomy. The epilogue consisted of liturgical versions of the oracles of four 8th century prophets, Hosea, Amos, Isaiah and Micah. The Deutero-nomic circle of Levitical priests and scribes which produced DH were influenced by the oracles of these 8th century prophets. Hosea and Amos had delivered the words of Yahweh to the decision makers of Samaria, and Isaiah and Micah had spoken for Yahweh to Jerusalem in addition to foretelling the destruction of Samaria. In this chapter we will make a brief statement about the origin and growth of these four prophets.

To Whom Were the Oracles of the Four 8th Century Prophets Addressed?

The oracles of the 8th century prophets were not addressed to the people of Israel/Judah *en masse*. The original oracles were ad-dressed to the rich and powerful elite, the decision makers of the capital cities of Samaria and Judah. For example, Hosea said:

Hear this, O priests!
Give heed, O house of Israel!
Listen, O house of the King!
For the judgement pertains to you (Hosea 5:1–2).

Amos addressed ". . . the people of Israel who dwell in Samaria"
(3:12), "house of Israel" (5:1), and "Those who are at ease in (original
word missing) and . . . those who feel secure on Mount Samaria"
(6:1). Isaiah spoke face to face with King Ahaz and King Hezekiah,
and Micah said:

Hear this, you rulers of the house of Jacob and chiefs of the
house of Israel, who abhor justice and pervert all equity,
who build Zion with blood and Jerusalem with wrong (Micah 3:9–10).

Oracles addressed to the powerful decision makers of Samaria and
Jerusalem constitute one of the chief characteristics for identifying
the original oracles of the 8th century.

Hosea[1]

The final (canonical) book of Hosea contains three editorial layers of text in addition to the original oracles of Hosea ben Berri. Gale
Yee in the book based on her dissertation, *Composition and Tradition in the Book of Hosea, A Redaction Critical Investigation*, states
that the original oracles of Hosea begin in chapter 2, verse 4:

Plead with your mother, plead—
that she put away her harlotry from her face,
and her adultery from between her breasts;
lest I strip her naked
and make her as in the day she was born,
and make her like a wilderness,
and set her like a parched land,
and slay her with thirst (2:2–3).

For Hosea, the sin of the decision makers of Samaria was in making
alliances with Egypt (and Syria) for protection against Assyria and
making alliances with Assyria for protection against Egypt, instead
of trusting in Israel's ancient relationship with Yahweh.

Ephraim (*Hosea's name for Israel*) has become like a dove,
    silly and without sense;
they call upon Egypt, they go to Assyria (Hosea 7:11).
Ephraim has bargained for lovers.
Though they bargain with the nations,
I will now gather them up.
They shall soon writhe under the burden of kings and princes
    (Hosea 8:9–10).

There was no mention of Gomer in the original oracles of Hosea. When Hosea spoke the following words he did not have Gomer in mind:

Plead with your mother plead—
that she put away her harlotry from her face,
and her adultery from between her breast;
lest I strip her naked
and make her like the day she was born,
and make her like a wilderness (Hosea 2:2–3).

He was speaking about Samaria and Ephraim, the reduced state of Israel, and he was referring to her political allies whom he referred to as hired lovers (Hosea 8:9).

When the Josianic edition of Hosea appeared as part of the postlude to DH, Israel, the northern kingdom, was long gone. The editor/scribe reinterpreted the sin of Israel. For the Josianic editor the sin of Israel was not political but cultic and legal. The Josianic redactor was concerned with two themes, cultic purity and obedience to the law.

They shall be ashamed because of their altars (Hosea 4:10).

When Ephraim multiplied altars to expiate sin,
they became to him altars for sinning (Hosea 8:11).[2]

All Josianic additions to the oracles of Hosea are in accordance with the Deuteronomic perception of Yahweh as a God who is preoccupied with cultic purity and obedience to the law which promotes cultic purity.

The final editorial layer of Hosea, the exilic portions, deal with the captivity circumstances of the defeated people of Israel/Judah.

The mercy of Yahweh is introduced. The names of the children of Hosea are changed from negative to positive, for example:

> And I will have pity on *Not pitied*
> and I will say to *Not my people*,
> "You are my people"(Hosea 1:10).

Israel desires to return to Yahweh:

> Then she shall say, "I will go and return to my first husband" (Hosea 2:7),

and Yahweh will say:

> And I will take you for my wife forever. . . . I will take you for my wife in faithfulness; and you shall know the LORD (Hosea 2:19–20).

The closing words of the canonical book of Hosea are from the wisdom genre and are either the contribution of the Josianic historian or the exilic editor:

> Those who are wise understand these things,
> those who are discerning know them [etc.] (Hosea 14:9).

Amos

The original oracles of Amos constitute 28 percent of the canonical book of Amos.[3] They begin with the words:

> . . . they sell the righteous for silver
> and the needy for a pair of sandals—
> they who trample the head of the poor into the dust of the
>   earth
> and push the afflicted out of the way (Amos 2:6–7).

and are found meaningfully placed throughout a liturgical framework created by a Josianic scribe of the Deuteronomic circle. All the original oracles are addressed to the powerful elite of Samaria. They have their foundation in the anger and suffering of the masses of Israel with whom Amos identified. Yahweh has not forgotten the poor and the powerless, so Samaria will be punished for her treatment of Yahweh's people whom Amos calls the righteous.[4] There is no hope for the callous oppressors of the poor in the oracles of Amos. His final words are:

> And though they go into captivity in front of their enemies,
> there I will command the sword, and it shall kill them (Amos
>   9:4).

The Josianic scribe of the late 7th century who placed the oracles of Amos into a liturgical structure had a fondness for the number five. It appealed to him as an appropriate liturgical number for public use. So, following the title verse, there can be found the first of five verses of a hymn scattered throughout the updated version of the book of Amos. The 7th century edition of Amos also contained five oracles against the nations (Damascus, Gaza, Ammon, Moab, and Israel). In the fifth oracle, against Israel, the first words of Amos appear.[5]

There is also a litany of five former judgements (Amos 4:6–11) which should have produced a return to Yahweh, each evoking the response:

> Yet you did not return to me, says the LORD.

Because the people did not return to Yahweh, they are warned:

> Prepare to meet your God, O Israel (Amos 4:12).

The 7th century scribe of Jerusalem addresses a different audience than the one addressed by Amos. Amos had addressed the elite decision makers of Samaria. The scribe addressed the people of Yahweh:

> I struck you with blight and mildew,
> I laid waste your gardens and your vineyards;
> the locust devoured your fig trees and your olive trees;
> yet you did not return to me, says the LORD (Amos 4:9).

The story of Amos' rejection by Amaziah at the shrine at Bethel (Amos 7:10–15) was crafted by the Josianic historian to serve the need of the Deuteronomic circle to completely discredit the shrine at Bethel, and to support Josiah's desecration and destruction of Bethel as a competing shrine to Jerusalem (2 Kings 23:15–20). In this

CHART 15
THREE LEVELS OF AUTHORSHIP IN THE OPENING CHAPTERS OF AMOS

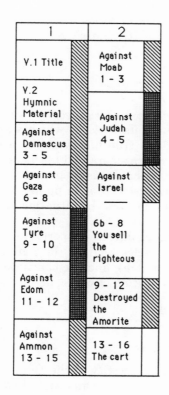

1	2
V.1 Title	Against Moab 1 - 3
V.2 Hymnic Material	Against Judah 4 - 5
Against Damascus 3 - 5	
Against Gaza 6 - 8	Against Israel ———
Against Tyre 9 - 10	6b - 8 You sell the righteous
Against Edom 11 - 12	9 - 12 Destroyed the Amorite
Against Ammon 13 - 15	13 - 16 The cart

AMOS A 8th Century

AMOS B 7th Century

AMOS C 6th Century

The original 8th century oracles of Amos are located throughout the canonical book of Amos beginning in chapter 2, verse 6b. There is 7th century material (Josianic) and 6th century material (exilic) surrounding the oracles of Amos, and providing a structure for the original oracles.

Amos tradition, Bethel becomes a place where a true prophet of
Yahweh was forbidden to speak the words of Yahweh. Amaziah says:

> O seer, go, flee away to the land of Judah . . . but never
> again prophesy at Bethel (Amos 7:12).

The most famous oracle from the book of Amos, based on the
spirit of Amos's oracles, was written by the 7th century scribe:

> But let justice roll down like waters
> and righteousness like a mighty stream (5:24).

Amos did not use abstract words like *justice* and *righteousness*.[6] In
delivering his original oracles, Amos only used words which were
concrete, specific and *down to earth*. It is true however that the
scribe was only the first of 2700 years of preachers and teachers of
righteousness, inspired by Amos, who have been unable to avoid the
use of generalizations like *justice* and *righteousness*. In public ritu-
als, it seems, general words are used to address the situation of a
diversity of hearers.

Following the destruction of Jerusalem, during the period of the
scattering of Judah, three additional oracles against the nations
were added to Amos (Edom, Tyre, and Judah), and the concluding
optimistic words which promise the restoration of peace, defined as
agricultural tranquility (Amos 9:11).

Isaiah of Jerusalem[7]

It is possible that without the scribal activity of the Deuteronomic circle we would not have the oracles of Hosea and Amos in our
scriptures. This is not true for Isaiah however. Isaiah was a Jerusalem prophet who spoke with kings. In one form or another the oracles of Isaiah would have become part of the recognized canon.[8] A
discussion of the complex growth of the canonical book of Isaiah is
completely beyond the purpose of this chapter.[9]

An early edition of Isaiah may have consisted of chapters 2
through 11, beginning with the words:

> The word that Isaiah son of Amoz saw concerning Judah
> and Jerusalem (Isaiah 2:1).[10]

A careful examination of this section indicates that an earlier collection of liturgical oracles were opened to insert the memoirs of Isaiah, chapter 6:1 to 8:18. The memoirs begin with Isaiah's vision of Yahweh:

> In the year that King Uzziah died, I saw the LORD sitting on a throne, high and lofty; and the hem of his robe filled the temple (6:1).

Some scholars believe that the vision of Isaiah was an inaugural call, while others believe that it was a call for Isaiah to become a different kind of prophet, a prophet who henceforth would speak to kings concerning matters of international importance. We note that social justice themes, similar to those of Amos, appear in the chapters before Isaiah's vision as chart 16 indicates:

The First Chapter of Isaiah

The first chapter of Isaiah is a later introduction to the book than the material found in chapters 2 through 12. The following passage could easily have been written by the Deuteronomic scribes during the period between the first capture of Jerusalem (597) and the final destruction (586).

> And daughter Zion is left like a booth in a vineyard,
>   like a shelter in a cucumber field,
>   like a besieged city.
> If the LORD of hosts had not left us a few survivors,
>   we would have been like Sodom and Gomorrah (Isaiah 1:8–
>   9).

Deuteronomic treaty language is found in chapter 1 of Isaiah when the LORD calls on heaven and earth to witness the rebellion and disobedience of Yahweh's people (Isaiah 1:2–4). In Deuteronomy we read:

> I call heaven and earth to witness against you today. . . .
> The LORD will scatter you among the people (Deuteronomy 4:26–27; see also 30:19; 31:28).

CHART 16
PARALLELS BETWEEN THE BOOK OF AMOS AND ISAIAH 2–5

SUBJECT	AMOS	ISAIAH
Oppression and abuse of the poor.	2:6-7; 5:11; 8:6	3:15
Words against the women of the capital cities.	4:1–3	3:16–24
Against drunkenness.	4:1; 6:6	5:11,22
Empty houses.	5:11	5:9
The Day of the LORD.	5:18–20	2:11ff
Corrupt administration of justice (bribes).	5:12	1:23; 10:1-2
Critical comments about instruments of music	5:23; 6:5	5:12
The LORD's displeasure with sacrificial offerings.	5:21–23	1:13–15

Just as the following powerful words now found in Amos were the work of a Deuteronomic Josianic redactor:

> Even though you offer me your burnt offerings and grain
>   offerings
>   I will not accept them;
> And the offerings of well-being of your fatted animals I will
>   not look upon (Amos 5:22),

so, the parallel passage in Isaiah Chapter 1 was also the work of the same Deuteronomic (Josianic) hand:

> What to me is the multitude of your sacrifices? says the
> LORD;
> I have had enough of burnt offerings of rams and the fat of
> fed beasts (Isaiah 1:11).

Isaiah is the only book of prophecy which contains portions of the Deuteronomistic History. Isaiah chapters 36 to 39 share three incidents with DH (2 Kings 18:13–20:19).

(a) The siege of Jerusalem and the speech by the Rabshakeh.
(b) Hezekiah's illness and recovery.
(c) The visit of the Babylonian envoy to Jerusalem.

These narratives were written and became part of Isaiah shortly after the appearance of the Josianic edition of DH, almost a hundred years after the death of Isaiah. The following words attributed to Isaiah (39:5–7) could have been written between 597, the first exile of Jerusalemites (2 Kings 24:13–17), involving members of the house of David, and 586, the date of the final destruction of the temple. Notice that no mention is made of the destruction of the temple:

> Days are coming when all that is in your house shall be
> carried to Babylon; nothing shall be left, says the LORD.
> Some of your own sons who are born to you shall be eunuchs
> in the palace of the king of Babylon (Isaiah 39:6–7).

Deutero-Isaiah and Trito-Isaiah

The oracles of Isaiah of Jerusalem are located in Isaiah Chapters 2 through 33. They are framed (bracketed) by Deuteronomistic sections consisting of Chapter 1 and the DH narrative of Chapters 36 through 39. (Chapters 34 and 35 are out of place. They are considered exilic oracles.)

Deutero-Isaiah (40 through 55) was influenced by Deuteronomistic ideas. Idolatry and foreign worship are attacked and singled out for ridicule. The unknown author was not a Deuteronomist or a direct heir of the Deuteronomic circle. The author was a member of the Babylonian Judahite community. I believe that the heirs of the Deuteronomic circle went to Egypt with some of its members possibly remaining in Judah.

Third Isaiah is a collection of post-exilic oracles. Many show the influence of Deuteronomistic theology. The editor was not a Deuteronomist however. As a cohesive group with a self-conscious group identity, I do not believe that the Deuteronomists survived into the restoration period.

Micah

Micah is the only 8th century prophet who has the distinction of being quoted by the 7th century prophet Jeremiah:

Micah of Moresheth, who prophesied during the days of King Hezekiah of Judah, said to all the people of Judah: "Thus says the LORD of hosts:
Zion shall be plowed as a field;
Jerusalem shall become a heap of ruins,
and the mountain of the house a wooded height" (Jeremiah 26:18).

Although Jeremiah says that Micah spoke to *all the people of Judah*, a reading of the original oracle of Micah shows that it was directed to the elite decision makers in positions of power, supporting our statement that the 8th century prophets addressed the politically powerful of the capital cities:

Hear this you rulers of the house of Jacob
   and chiefs of the house of Israel,
who abhor justice and pervert all equity,
   who build Zion with blood and Jerusalem with wrong
     (Micah 3:9–10).

Like Amos, Micah is very specific when he speaks to issues of economic injustice which he experiences:

. . . you rise against my people as an enemy;
you strip the robe from the peaceful,
. . . . the women of my people you drive out of their pleasant
    houses;
and from their young children you take away my glory
    forever (Micah 2:8–9).

A century later, the Josianic editor of Micah added the words below. He perceived of Yahweh as a God who was obsessed with obedience to the law (the torah) and social order:[11]

> He has told you, O mortal, what is good;
> and what does the LORD require of you
> but to do justice, and to love kindness,
> and to walk humbly with your God (Micah 6:8)?

This same Josianic editor de-emphasizes the importance of animal sacrifice, as he did in Amos and Isaiah:

> Shall I come before him with burnt offerings,
> and calves a year old?
> Will the LORD be pleased with thousands of rams,
> with ten thousand rivers of oil (Micah 6:7)?

Almost a century later the exilic editor would add these words, promising restoration and return to Jerusalem:

> In that day, says the LORD,
> I will assemble the lame
> and gather those who have been driven away,
> and those whom I have afflicted.
> The lame I will make the remnant,
> and those who were cast off, a strong nation;
> and the LORD will reign over them in Mount Zion
> now and forevermore (Micah 4:6–7).

Conclusion

The 8th century prophets are best understood if the student is aware that there is Josianic editorial material (DTR 1) and exilic editorial material (DTR 2) throughout the canonical versions.

It is because of the great value which the Deuteronomic circle placed on the oracles of the 8th century prophets that we have their oracles preserved for us in the Hebrew Bible. This brings us to the subject of the heritage of the Deuteronomic circle.

CHART 17
DIVISION OF THE BOOK OF MICAH*

CHAPTERS	CONTENT
1 TO 3	The original oracles of Micah, delivered in the days of Hezekiah, are found here. Micah's oracles, like those of Amos, contain rage directed against powerful urban decision makers (in Samaria and Jerusalem) because of exploitation of the rural poor.
4 TO 5	This section is exilic (Babylonian). The oracles are filled with hope for the exiles. This collection ends with anti-idolatry polemic (5:12–15).
6 TO 7	This section contains both Josianic (6:7–8) and late or post-exilic redaction. It contains elements of the vassal treaty metaphor introduced by the Deuteronomists during the exile. It closes with a liturgy of faith (7:8–20).

* This division of the book of Micah based on style and subject matter is espoused by many scholars including James L. Mays, Bruce T. Dahlberg, David Hagstrom, and others.

NOTES

1. In addition to the work of Gale Yee referred to in the text (see also Bibliography) see *Prophet of Love, Understanding the Book of Hosea*, by William J. Doorly (Mahwah: Paulist Press, 1991).

2. Notice that Ephraim is masculine in this verse, ". . . they became to him altars for sinning," whereas Hosea referred to Israel as female, "I will strip her naked and expose her as in the day she was born" (2:3).

3. Consult Robert Coote's book *Amos Among the Prophets* (Philadelphia: Fortress Press, 1979).

4. Consult *Prophet of Justice, Understanding the Book of Amos*, by William Doorly (Mahwah: Paulist Press, 1989).

5. Almost all scholars agree that three oracles against the nations currently found in Amos were added later, probably during the exile. These are oracles against Edom, Tyre, and Judah. Their form differs from the form of the earlier five.

6. See *Amos Among the Prophets*, by Robert B. Coote, page 63.

7. It is generally agreed upon that the oracles of Isaiah of Jerusalem are found located in the first 33 chapters of Isaiah. The first 39 chapters are referred to as First Isaiah. Consult the articles on Isaiah in the *New Jerome Biblical Commentary*.

8. While it is the premise of this book that the Deuteronomic circle first produced and recognized the written word as a new form of revelation from Yahweh, inevitably (probably during the scattering of the people of Judah) this development would have become a reality.

9. For advanced students we recommend the *New Century Bible Commentary, Isaiah 1–39*, by R.E. Clements (Grand Rapids: Eerdmans, 1987). The sections on Isaiah in the *New Jerome Biblical Commentary* are very helpful. Another Paulist Press book treating the subject of the growth of Isaiah is *Isaiah of Jerusalem* by William J. Doorly.

10. This is a title of oracles which follow, but it is not an accurate title. Some of the oracles contained in this early collection are directed to the northern kingdom of Israel.

11. Read Deuteronomy 10:12: "So now, O Israel, what does the LORD require of you? Only to fear the LORD your God, to walk in all his ways . . . to keep the commandments of the LORD your God."

Chapter 12

THE HERITAGE OF THE
DEUTERONOMIC CIRCLE

There is no doubt that the decision to produce an authoritative collection of scrolls during the reign of Josiah, promoting the nationalization of Judah and supporting the centralization of Yahwism in Jerusalem, had the effect of standardizing a form of Yahwism. In Israel's past there had been many forms of Yahwism as the variety of local traditions, written and oral, indicates. There were urban and rural differences and there were northern and southern variations.

In their scrolls, the Deuteronomic circle created the impression that they were restoring the golden age of Israel's relationship with Yahweh. The wilderness experience was colored by images of a parent and child relationship and a husband and wife relationship. This has been called the positive wilderness experience.

> When Israel was a child, I loved him. . . .
> It was I who taught Ephraim to walk,
> I took them up in my arms (Hosea 11:1–3).

And in Deuteronomy we read:

> . . . and in the wilderness, where you saw how the LORD your God carried you, just as one carries a child (Deuteronomy 1:31).

On the plains of Moab, Moses was presented as being able to address the leaders and citizens of a united Israel which could not have existed in those ancient times, hundreds of years before the

CHART 18
TYPICAL DTR 1 (JOSIANIC) THEMES OR PHRASES

1.	. . . to this day	2 Kings 17:34; Joshua 9:27; Joshua 16:63; 1 Samuel 27:26; and others.
2.	. . . not turning to the right hand or to the left.	Joshua 1:7; 2 Kings 22:2.
3.	. . . the place chosen for my *name* to dwell.	1 Kings 8:29; 8:44; 11:36; 2 Kings 21:4; 21:7.
4.	David and the Davidic promise.	1 Kings 8:16; 11:12; 15:4; 2 Kings 8:19; 20:6.
5.	. . . the sin(s) of Jeroboam.	1 Kings 16:31; 2 Kings 10:29; 13:6; 14:24; 15:9; 17:22.
6.	. . . the king did not remove the *high places.*	1 Kings 15:14; 22:43; 2 Kings 12:3; 14:4; 15:35; and others.

TYPICAL DTR 2 (EXILIC) THEMES OR PHRASES

1.	Heaven and earth called as witnesses.	Deut 4:26; 30:19; 31:28.
2.	*Scattering* of the people	Deut 4:27; 28:64; 30:3; 1 Kings 14:15.
3.	Compassion (*racham*) of Yahweh	Deut 4:31; 30:3; 1 Kings 8:50.
4.	Turn or return to Yahweh	Deut 30:2; 30:8; Hosea 6:1; 14:1; 1 Kings 8:33; 8:48.
5.	Egypt called the *house of bondage.*	Deut 13:10; Joshua 24:17; Judges 6:8.
6.	Nations ask why Yahweh has devastated this land (city).	Deut 29:24; 1 Kings 9:8; Jeremiah 22:8.

monarchy. The Deuteronomic circle was not restoring a golden age; they were in fact creating such an age.[1]

Vital decisions had to be made concerning proper and acceptable forms of religious behavior, and Yahweh was perceived of by these priests and scribes as being preoccupied with cultic purity and obedience to the law.

> When you cross the Jordan to go in to occupy the land . . .
> you must diligently observe all the statutes and ordinances
> that I am setting before you today (Deuteronomy 11:31).

At the same time Yahweh was perceived by this circle as not being interested in the details of the complicated sacrificial system and endless matters related to ceremonial uncleanness as later detailed in the tetrateuch. And even circumcision was not commanded by the Deuteronomic torah.[2]

Religious practices which the Deuteronomic torah condemned were identified as Amorite, Canaanite, Moabite and Assyrian.

> . . . do not inquire concerning their gods. . . . You must not
> do the same for the Lord your God, because every abhorrent
> thing that the LORD hates they have done for their gods.
> They would even burn their sons and daughters in the fire
> to their gods (Deuteronomy 12:30–32).

The first Israelites were the indigenous people of the land, many of whom had moved into the central highlands to escape the exploitation of the city-state system which lined the trade routes between Egypt and Assyria. As time went by they were joined by other marginal groups from the east and south during the 200 year period preceding the monarchy. When the loose federation of rural clans first adopted Yahweh as a warrior god who would fight for second-class citizens, so-called Canaanite religious practices continued. Following the establishment of the monarchy a new variety of foreign religious beliefs and practices entered the picture.[3] These practices (Canaanite, Jebusite and Assyrian) competed with emerging forms of Yahwism.

The prohibitions of the Deuteronomic torah and the reforms of Josiah indicate that many diverse religious practices survived in Jerusalem into the late 7th century. The reformation had to deal with the prohibition of child sacrifice, participation in fertility rites, communication with the dead, worship of stars and planets, and

devotion to Baal and Asherah to name some of the practices which
the Deuteronomic torah prohibited.

The decisions made by the Deuteronomic circle and the Deuteronomists conformed to a principle which has resulted in the survival of
the religion of Israel. They promoted practices which enhanced the
dignity of humans and the majesty of God. To give an example, unlike
the competing Aaronid priesthood they diminished the anthropomor-
phism of Aaronid belief.[4] For the Deuteronomists, Yahweh did not
dwell in the temple as these words attributed to Solomon indicate:

> The LORD has said that he would dwell in thick darkness. I
> have built you an exalted house, a place for you to dwell
> forever (1 Kings 8:12–12).

The Deuteronomic scribes made it clear that only *the name* of Yahweh dwelt in the temple:

> But will God indeed dwell on the earth? Even heaven and
> the highest heaven cannot contain you much less this house
> that I have built (1 Kings 8:27).

The worship of Yahweh and Yahweh alone was the undeniable goal
of the DH.

> Hear, O Israel: The LORD (Yahweh) is our God, the LORD
> alone (Deuteronomy 6:4).

Without doubt, the promotion of one God for Israel was the giant
step in the direction of monotheism.

New Meaning for the Exodus

We do not know the role played in Israel/Judah of the exodus
tradition before the destruction of Jerusalem and the scattering of
the people.[5] The 8th century prophets had little to say about the
exodus, and the Josianic historian started his history with the people ending their wilderness experience, about to enter the land.

We do know that a new age of exodus-based theology started
when the exilic editor (called DTR 2 by many scholars) updated the
Josianic edition of DH and added numerous references to the fact
that Yahweh had led his people out of Egypt. For the scattered peo-

ple of Judah, Egypt obviously meant Babylon *or* Egypt and exodus became the symbol of great hope for a devastated people. The majestic poet of the exile (Second Isaiah) would further develop this renewed exodus theme, and, following the exile, the priestly party would formulate a new, powerful exodus scroll by merging J and E (a northern version of J) in its own narrative and theological structure. But it was the Deuteronomist who first recognized its vital value. In the earliest version of the ten commandments we first read:

> I am the LORD your God who brought you out of the land of Egypt, out of the house of slavery; you shall have no other gods before me (Deuteronomy 5:6).

Liturgy and Words

> Take words with you and return to the LORD.
> Say to him, "Take away all guilt:
> accept that which is good,
> and we will offer you the fruit of our lips" (Hosea 14:2–3).

The above is a Deuteronomistic addition to the scroll of Hosea. The practice of the Deuteronomic scribes, placing the oracles of the 8th century prophets in a form for public reading and response, made these scribes the first liturgists of the Judeo-Christian tradition.[6] This was the first step in the transformation of the temple of Yahweh from a place of animal sacrifice to a house of prayer. In Deuteronomy words to be spoken by the presenter of offerings are supplied, including the following:

> Look down from your holy habitation from heaven, and bless your people Israel and the ground you have given us, as you swore to our ancestors—a land flowing with milk and honey (Deuteronomy 26:15).

In the tetrateuch the offerings are made without words, in silence.

Following the destruction of Jerusalem, during the exilic period, the people of Yahweh became people of the word wherever they found themselves. Reading, listening, understanding became the essence of their religion.[7] If there is one word which is characteristic of the religion of Deuteronomy it is the word *hear*.

Hear, O Israel: The LORD thy God is one (Deuteronomy 6:4).

Numerous passages in Deuteronomy can be cited:

. . . the LORD said to me (Moses), "Assemble the people for me, and I will let them hear my words" (Deuteronomy 4:10).

Words and Prophets

The masses of Israel did not read. Public reading of the words of Yahweh started during the reign of Josiah. In order for the people to be held responsible for not keeping the law of Yahweh (during the centuries before Josiah) the exilic editor had to introduce the important role of the prophets who spoke the words of Yahweh to the people. Without the Deuteronomistic history we would know very little about the prophets. The second history of Israel which appears in the Bible (Chronicles, Ezra, Nehemiah) does not report in detail the vital role which the prophets played in the nation's history. In Chronicles Elijah and Elisha are ignored;[8] only a few prophets are referred to.[9]

Without the scribal activity of the Deuteronomic circle of the late 7th century we would not have the oracles of the 8th century prophets. In Amos we read this editorial comment:

Surely the LORD does nothing, without revealing his secret to his servants the prophets (Amos 3:7).

DH legitimized the central role of the prophet in Israel, preparing the way for the acceptance of later literary prophets such as Jeremiah, Ezekiel, and Second and Third Isaiah. In an exilic passage designed to place the blame for the fall of Israel on the shoulders of the people (rather than the kings) we read:

. . . the LORD warned Israel and Judah by every prophet and every seer,[10] saying, "Turn from your evil ways and keep my commandments and my statutes . . . that I sent to you by my servants the prophets" (1 Kings 17:13).

In considering the heritage of the Deuteronomists we should not forget the obvious, the Deuteronomistic history itself. The books

Joshua, Judges, Samuel, and Kings (along with Deuteronomy and the Deuteronomic update of the four 8th century prophets) became the heart of the Hebrew Bible. Many years after their appearance, four books (the tetrateuch) were placed before DH and many others were added following DH.

Although DH was not pure history in a modern sense, it has preserved for us the many primary sources referred to in chapter 5 on the four layers of authorship and a primary theology of two distinct periods, the Josianic period and the exile.

Faith and Faithfulness

The Deuteronomic circle was composed of a small number of Levitical priests and scribes in Jerusalem during the reign of Josiah, with deep roots in the former northern kingdom of Israel. That they were able to produce the Josianic edition of DH was a massive, herculean task in itself. After the death of Josiah and the rapid decline of Judah resulting in its complete destruction, the heirs of this circle found themselves powerless and uprooted. That they were able to completely re-edit and recompose their previous effort, now rendered obsolete, is one of the greatest examples of the triumph of faith over despair which the world has ever witnessed. With no wealth, no influence, and no political power whatsoever the Deuteronomists produced one of the greatest examples of world literature, the Deuteronomistic history with its introduction, Deuteronomy, and postlude, exilic editions of four 8th century prophets. This collection of writings has influenced and inspired its readers for over 2500 years, and the end of its powerful influence on humankind is not in sight.

NOTES

1. See Saul M. Olyan, *Asherah and the Cult of Yahweh in Israel*, page 9; also, Robert B. Coote, *Early Israel*, page 6 and chapter 4, "Israel in the Thirteenth Century."

2. The only time circumcision is mentioned in the book of Deuteronomy it is referred to as circumcision of the heart (10:16 and 30:6).

3.   For example, it is reported that Ahaz moved an altar in the temple, made in the days of Solomon, to make room for a foreign altar which he copied during a trip to Syria to show respect for the Assyrian king Tiglath-pileser (2 Kings 16:10–11).

4.   See Moshe Weinfeld, *Deuteronomy 1–11*, pages 37–38.

5.   The J document contained detailed information about the exodus experience of the Hebrews. The J document, before being incorporated into the tetrateuch by the heirs of the Aaronid priestly party after the exile, may have had a very limited circulation. Robert Coote states that the J account of ancient times served the purposes of legitimating the early house of David. See Coote's *Early Israel* (Philadelphia: Fortress, 1990), pages 156–161.

6.   Read chapter 26 of Deuteronomy for verbal responses to be used by worshipers at the time of the offerings of first fruits.

7.   Read chapter 3, "Assembling for Worship and Instruction," in Carroll Stuhlmueller's book *New Paths Through the Old Testament* (Mahwah: Paulist Press, 1989), pages 39–54.

8.   Elijah is mentioned once in Chronicles as writing a letter to King Jehoram (2 Chronicles 21:11–17).

9.   One example of a prophet's role in Chronicles is the role of Micaiah in the court of Ahab of Israel (2 Chronicles 18). This, however, is not typical of the Chronicles history.

10.   Samuel had the title seer. In 1 Samuel 9:9 we read this editorial comment: . . . the one who is now called a prophet (*nabi*) was formerly called a seer (*ra'ah*).

In the middle of the 13th century, Israel emerged in the High-lands, a mountainous area running north and south from Gali-lee to the Negev, west of the Jordan Valley, and east of the coastal plains of the Great Sea.

Some villages and cities which later became important in Israel are named in the above map.

Israel was a small nation surrounded by other small nations, each with its own god.

Chapter 13

GOING BACK TO THE BEGINNING

Israel existed for 200 years as a loose federation of subsistence farming communities in an area less than ideal for farming. This was possible only because of the emergence of interrelated social institutions such as the extended family, clans, and tribes. Survival by subsistence farming took place because groups at various levels were able to work together to share resources and risks.[1] The tribes of Israel had the following common characteristics:

1. They called the highlands their home.
2. They were chiefly subsistence farmers and herders.
3. They lived in a contiguous area.
4. They shared the same functional social institutions.
5. All Israelites came from the margins of a more affluent society. They saw themselves as marginal people.
6. They shared and traded each other's traditions.
7. Although the first God of Israel was El, a chief god of the Canaanites, Yahweh emerged as their favorite God, a warrior-god who championed the causes of the under-classes of society.

Norman Gottwald in *The Tribes of Yahweh*[2] speaks of the functionality of a growing acknowledgement of and devotion to Yahweh and calls it mono-Yahwism. Mono-Yahwism was a theological perception which provided for these heterogeneous groups a growing cohesion which would not otherwise have been possible.

Continued existence of proto-Israel as a completely rural society for 200 years was only possible because there was no apparent need for a center of political power. In pre-monarchical Israel there was no strong city-state to dominate or exploit the surrounding rural areas.

The need for a monarchy did not spring into existence in an instant. The idea of monarchy surfaced from time to time in traditions preserved in Judges, stories of Gideon, Abimelech, and possibly Jephthah. Although Saul, a Benjaminite, is recognized as the first king of Israel, it was not until David captured the Jebusite fortress, Jerusalem, that the monarchy began to take on the characteristics of the ancient near eastern monarchy and a powerful urban culture began to emerge. The original city of Jerusalem (sometimes called Jebus, Zion or Salem) was small and later became known as the City of David. The capital began to grow immediately by extensions of the walls, and under Solomon, whose massive building program is well known to us, continued to grow in size and population. In support of the monarchy the urban population of Jerusalem grew rapidly.

The reward for David's supporters was a higher standard of living than they had ever experienced before. And many supporters were needed. An urban power structure began to emerge immediately, including military advisors and generals, administrators, functionaries, bureaucrats, and an official priesthood for a newly emerging form of urban religion, with a theological viewpoint which would support the house of David.

Jerusalem continued to grow. Solomon conducted a massive building program:

> In the fourth year of Solomon's reign he began to build the house of the LORD. . . . Solomon was building his own house thirteen years. . . . He built the House of the Forest of Lebanon. . . . He made the Hall of Pillars. . . . He made the Hall of the Throne. . . . He also made a house like this hall for Pharaoh's daughter (1 Kings 6:1–7:8).

For his building program Solomon needed an unlimited supply of forced labor:

> King Solomon conscripted forced labor out of Israel; the levy numbered thirty thousand men. . . . Solomon also had seventy thousand laborers and eighty thousand stonecutters in the hill country, besides Solomon's three thousand three hundred supervisors (1 Kings 4:13–16).

A pro-Solomonic statement appears in 1 Kings 9:22 where we read ". . . but of the Israelites Solomon made no slaves." The overwhelming evidence however is that Solomon conscripted large numbers of Israelites from the rural areas for corvée labor.[3]

Urban Theology

For the first 200 years of its existence Israel had been completely rural. Immediately after the establishment of Jerusalem as the new capital city, an new urban form of Yahwism began to emerge. This new form of Yahwism combined pre-Israelite (Jebusite) concepts concerning the sacredness of Zion with ancient Israelite concepts concerning the uniqueness of Yahweh as the special warrior God of the Israelites. An understanding of a special relationship between Yahweh and the house of David became the core belief of what would later be called *royal theology*.

One way for a dense population to live a luxurious life within a walled city-state, enjoying a variety of fruit, grain, and meat, while not engaging in farming, was to control and exploit the surrounding farming community. When there was a desire to conduct a massive building program, a large amount of slave labor was needed. In a speech attributed to Samuel describing a near eastern monarchy we read:

> He will take your daughters to be perfumers and cooks and bakers. He will take the best of your fields. . . . He will take one tenth of your grain and of your vineyards and give it to his officers and his courtiers. He will take . . . the best of your cattle and donkeys and put them to his work. He will take one tenth of your flocks and you will be his slaves (1 Samuel 8:13–17).

After Jerusalem was established as a city-state, international trade became possible.

> King Solomon built a fleet of ships at Ezion-geber. . . . Hiram sent his servants with the fleet, sailors who were familiar with the sea, together with the servants of Solomon. They went to Ophir, and imported four hundred twenty talents of gold, which they delivered to King Solomon (1 Kings 9:26–28).

CHART 19
ANTITHETICAL TRAITS OF CITY AND COUNTRYSIDE
IN ANCIENT ISRAEL FROM *THE TRIBES OF YAHWEH*
BY NORMAN GOTTWALD[4]

CITY	COUNTRYSIDE
urbanism	village life
maximum division of labor	minimum division of labor
social stratification	tendency toward class leveling
imposed quasi-feudal social relations	contractual or kin egalitarian social relations
political hierarchy	diffused and limited government
military imperialism	non-cooperation and military self-defense
latifundist agriculture	agriculture by autonomous peasants
commercialism	barter trade
concentration of surplus wealth in a sociopolitical elite	direct and equal consumption of wealth by the immediate producers of wealth

When the rural farming community which had been Israel was coerced into producing products for international trade (oil, wine, and grain) at the same time that manpower and womenpower from the rural areas was conscripted for royal military expeditions and other purposes in support of the monarchy and the city-state of Jerusalem, the unfair burdens placed on the back of Israel's rural population became unbearable. At the time of Solomon's death the non-urban population demanded a voice in controlling its own life.

The Levitical Priesthood of Shechem

Solomon's son Rehoboam went to Shechem to become king of all Israel (1 Kings 12:1). Why did Rehoboam go to Shechem, of all places, to become king? Jerusalem was the capital city and the only logical location for his coronation. This is a reasonable question. A reasonable answer is that the Levitical priests of Shechem (the ancestors of the Deuteronomic circle) spoke for the non-urban masses of Israel. Not only were these Levitical priests zealous for Yahweh, but they also were champions of justice and had a strong social agenda. They could not conceive of the God of Israel, who had delivered his people from captivity in Egypt and had fought for them against their enemies for centuries, as being willing to accept the current bondage of his people. They could not conceive of Yahweh as withdrawing from his relationship with Israel, forgetting his people, and happily dwelling in thick darkness in the royal temple of Jerusalem (1 Kings 8:12–13). Because of the reputation of these Levitical priests with the masses, they were looked upon by the farmers of Israel to speak for them at Shechem, and Rehoboam had no alternative but to come to Shechem.

When Rehoboam arrived in Shechem he was charged as follows:

Your father made our yoke heavy. Now therefore lighten the hard service of your father and his heavy yoke that he placed on us, and we will serve you (1 Kings 12:4).

We are not supplied with information which could be considered *historical* concerning the rise of Jeroboam, an Ephraimite, to become the first official monarch of the northern kingdom. Instead we have *a story* of the prophet Ahijah of Shiloh ripping his new garment into twelve pieces (see chapter 2). We do know that earlier Solomon had given Jeroboam charge over the forced labor of the house of Joseph (1

Kings 11:28). Whatever Jeroboam did after his appointment by Solomon, it made it necessary for him to flee for his life. He went to Egypt and did not return until Solomon's son, Rehoboam, went to Shechem to negotiate for the northern tribes. Whatever Jeroboam did led him to be chosen as king in Shechem. He obviously was considered a hero among his people.

> Then Jeroboam built Shechem in the hill country of Ephraim, and resided there (1 Kings 13:25).

Scholars tell us that Shechem, located between the mountains of Gerizim and Ebal, was an ancient cult center for El, Baal, and eventually Yahweh.[5] Shechem was on the main road from Jerusalem to the north, and was considered to be the center of Canaan. It would have been the ideal place for a capital city to rival Jerusalem. But then, without any detailed information being supplied, we are told the following:

> . . . he (Jeroboam) went out from there and built Penuel (1 Kings 12:25).

There are two questions crying out for answers here. (1) Why did Jeroboam leave Shechem? (2) Why is there no reason given concerning this move? The answer to the first question may be found in several later verses. Jeroboam had a split with the Levitical priests of Shechem.

> Jeroboam appointed priests among the people, who were not Levites (1 Kings 12:31).

A later passage gives us more information:

> . . . Jeroboam did not turn from his evil ways, but made priests for the high places again from among all the people; any who wanted to be priests he consecrated for the high places (1 Kings 13:33).

Why is the reader (listener, supposing that DH was read in public gatherings) supplied with no detailed information concerning the split between Jeroboam and the Levitical priests of Shechem? The answer is twofold.

(1) If the Deuteronomic circle was made up of the descendants of

the Levitical priestly circle of Shechem, now located in Jerusalem, as we are contending, the scribes of the circle did not want to present their ancestors as the leaders of a cult center which was a rival to Jerusalem. One of the main purposes of DH was to standardize and centralize the worship of Yahweh in the city of Jerusalem, *the place Yahweh chose for his name to dwell*. Even the story of Ahijah announcing the will of Yahweh to Jeroboam (before he fled to Egypt) contained these words:

> David shall always have a lamp before me in Jerusalem, the city where I have chosen to put my name (1 Kings 11:36).

It would not make sense to remind the reader that if Jeroboam had stayed in Shechem, Shechem would have been the chief rival to the city of Jerusalem, instead of Bethel, the desecration and destruction of which was targeted by the Deuteronomists.

(2) We have suggested previously that the Deuteronomic circle took pains to keep a low profile in putting together its history of Israel. The failure to mention the reason Jeroboam left Shechem was not an oversight, but a strategic decision by the priests, scribes, and prophets of the Deuteronomic circle to avoid raising issues about their own role which may have blurred the pursuit of their primary goal. It was in keeping with this strategy that no mention was made of Jeremiah in the history (DH), even though Jeremiah was the most influential member of the circle, if not the leader of the movement.

Jeroboam left Shechem because he could not have become the type of monarch he wanted to be as long as he was in the territory of this priesthood with its strong social agenda. These priests were zealous for Yahweh, and, like Yahweh, championed the cause of the common people, the lower classes of society. As soon as Jeroboam had time to think things over he realized that the eastern monarchy could not exist without the exploitation of the masses. So he severed his relationship with Shechem and started his own priesthood.

The best thing that happened to the Levitical priests of Shechem was their rejection by Jeroboam. This break with the monarch allowed them to develop their theology as a fringe group in the society of Israel, without the need of supporting the urban elite and the power structure which later developed in and around the monarchy. *Contrary to many recent books on the emergence of the Hebrew Bible, our viewpoint is that the scriptures of the Deuteronomists developed outside the power structure of both Samaria and Jerusalem.*

These scriptures were not royal propaganda to support a theology favorable to the elite ruling class. From the break with Jeroboam (approximately 925 B.C.E.) until the reign of Josiah of Judah (640 B.C.E.), for a period of 285 years, the theology of the Deuteronomists was developing outside the realm of the official state government. This is what made possible the development of economic justice as a major plank in the Deuteronomic platform.

Jeremiah

In chapter 3 we suggested that the theological ancestors of the Deuteronomic circle could be traced to the areas of Shiloh and Shechem. We discussed the role of Ahijah the Shilonite prophet, the activity at Shiloh of Samuel, the ideal Deuteronomic prophet, and the words of Jeremiah concerning Shiloh:

Shiloh . . . where I made my name dwell at first (Jeremiah 7:12).

The role of Shechem has been discussed in connection with the tradition of the journey of Rehoboam, Solomon's son, to Shechem to negotiate for the throne of Israel. In the book of Joshua, Joshua's activity is frequently reported to have been at Shechem or Shiloh.

During the reign of Josiah, the foremost proponent of the Shiloh/Shechem tradition was Jeremiah. Jeremiah is the only prophet to mention Shiloh (four times) and the only prophet to mention Samuel, making him an equal to Moses (Jeremiah 15:1). There is no doubt that Jeremiah was at the center of the Deuteronomic circle and its scribal output. Scholars have long asked the question, "Why is there no mention of Jeremiah in the Deuteronomistic history?" Our answer is that the author(s) of DH made a logistical, judgmental decision to keep himself (themselves) out of the history. In a recent scholarly work on DH we read, "The author at no point in the narrative reveals his identity to the reader."[6] We may reason that if the author of DH had been anyone else but Jeremiah he would have had to include Jeremiah's activity during the reign of Josiah and that the exilic editor would have had to include Jeremiah's activity in the account of the reigns of the kings following Josiah's death, as reported extensively in the book of Jeremiah (especially Jehoiakim and Zedekiah). The total absence of any mention of Jeremiah by the historian and the exilic editor supports the hypothesis that Jeremiah made a decision to keep himself out of the narrative.

An interesting possibility is raised by a study of the influence of DH on the formation of the later Chronicles' history. Steven Mc-Kenzie in his monograph *The Chronicler's Use of the Deutero-nomistic History* states that only the Josianic version of DH was used by the Chronicler.[7] This suggests that Judahites taken into captivity in 597 carried a Josianic version of DH to Babylon which began a life of its own apart from the exilic version of DH which was probably produced in Judah or Egypt. Knowing that Jeremiah and Baruch fled to Egypt in 585 (Jeremiah 41), following the assassination of Gedaliah, leads us to believe that Jeremiah and Baruch produced the exilic version of DH in Egypt.[8] That Egypt, Jeremiah's final home, may have been the location of DTR 2 is supported by R. E. Friedman who writes, "Whatever the situation with regard to authorship, the Deuteronomistic history in its final form tells the story of Israel from Egypt to Egypt."[9]

Following the assassination of Gedaliah we read:

> And all the people, young and old, and the officers of the soldiers arose and came to Egypt, for they feared the Babylonians (2 Kings 25:26).

The book of Jeremiah makes it clear that Jeremiah and Baruch produced scrolls, scrolls important enough to be inspected and destroyed by the king of Judah (Jeremiah 36). While we do not know the size of the Deuteronomic circle, there are names that we can cite. Gedaliah, the Babylonian-appointed governor of Judah, whom Jeremiah and Baruch followed to Mizpah, was the grandson of Shaphan the secretary. It was Shaphan who read the book of the law (*sepher hattorah*) in the presence of King Josiah. Shaphan was a scribe who could have helped with production of the Josianic version of DH. Ahikam, Gedaliah's father, supported Jeremiah and saved him from being stoned (Jeremiah 26:24). And an ancient Jewish tradition states that Jeremiah was the author of Kings.

Of course we must remember that there is no mention of a Deuteronomic circle in the Bible. This is a term which scholars have invented. It is not outside the realm of possibility, as we have suggested elsewhere, that Jeremiah and Baruch, preserving the traditions and values of the ancient Shechem/Shiloh Levitical priesthood, along with the use of additional primary sources (see chart 4), may have produced both the Josianic version and the exilic version of DH by themselves with only the support of a few friends.[10]

In our closing chapter we will examine the strong themes of social justice which run through the scriptures of the Deuteronomic circle and the exilic Deuteronomists.

NOTES

1.   Read chapters 9 and 10 of *The Highlands of Canaan, Agricultural Life in the Early Iron Age*, by David Hopkins.

2.   Read Norman K. Gottwald's *The Tribes of Yahweh* (Maryknoll: Orbis, 1979), pages 591–666.

3.   After Solomon's death the northern Israelites refused to continue bearing the burdens which Solomon had put on them. After Solomon's death we are told, "When King Rehoboam sent Adoram, who was taskmaster over the forced labor, all Israel stoned him to death."

4.   See page 462 and the surrounding text of *The Tribes of Yahweh* by Norman Gottwald (Maryknoll: Orbis Press, 1979).

5.   See *The New Jerome Biblical Commentary* (1990), page 1193.

6.   *Narrative History and Ethnic Boundaries*, by E. T. Mullen, Jr., page 92.

7.   Steven L. McKenzie, *The Chronicler's Use of the Deuteronomistic History* (Atlanta: Scholars Press, 1984), Chapter 6, pages 181 to 210. McKenzie suggests that the Chronicler depended on sources other than DH for his accounts of the kings following Josiah's death.

8.   Nelson, in *The Double Redaction of the Deuteronomistic History,* states that the phrase ". . . Egypt, the house of bondage," was not used by the Josianic historian, but was added to Deuteronomy and DH during the exile (Deuteronomy 5:6; 6:12; 26:10; Joshua 24:17; Judges 6:8).

9. *The Exile and Biblical Narrative*, page 36.

10. Many scholars believe that the starting point for DH was a short history of Israel which appeared during the reign of Hezekiah. For example see Baruch Halpern, *"The Editions of Kings in the 7th-6th Centuries B.C.E."*

Chapter 14

JUSTICE THEMES AND THE DEUTERONOMISTS

The original oracles of the 8th century prophet, Amos of Tekoa,[1] were entirely concerned with issues of economic justice. Amos accused the powerful elite of Samaria of exploiting and abusing the poor of the land for their own comfort and enrichment. The passionate concern of Amos was identical to that of the rural Levitical priests who preserved his oracles and carried them to Jerusalem following the destruction of the northern kingdom (which Amos had predicted). In the days of Josiah, as part of their goal and opportunity to educate and unite the people of Jerusalem and Judah, the descendants of the northern priests prepared a 7th century edition of Amos for public reading. If they had not done this we would probably not have the oracles of Amos today.

The 7th century edition of Amos opened with five oracles against the nations (Aram, Philistia, Ammon, Moab, and Israel). Oracles against the nations were attention-getters, and the masses who gathered for public liturgy expected them. Isaiah had written oracles against the nations (Isaiah 13–23). Each nation is accused of cruelty for which punishment is announced. These words are directed to Edom.

> . . . because he pursued his brother with the sword
> and cast off all pity;
> he maintained his anger perpetually,
> and kept his wrath forever.
> So I will send a fire on Teman,
> and it shall devour the strongholds of Bozrah (Amos 1:11–12).

When the oracle against Israel is presented in Amos, the cruelty is not performed by Israel against another nation. Instead the actual words of Amos are introduced (for the first time in the scroll) accusing the rich and powerful of Samaria of abusing and exploiting the poor of the land.

> . . . because they sell the righteous for silver
> and the needy for a pair of sandals—
> they who trample the head of the poor into the dust of the
>   earth,
> and push the afflicted out of the way (Amos 2:6–7).

This structure for the oracles of Amos was provided by a Deuteronomic scribe of the 7th century.[2]

The same themes of economic justice, or injustice, appear in the oracles of Isaiah (chiefly before the vision of Isaiah, in chapters 2–5). The social justice oracles of Isaiah 2–5 were preserved for us by the Deuteronomic circle.

When Amos delivered his original oracles he did not expect a response, nor did he challenge the people. The scribes of the Deuteronomic circle changed this however. It was a 7th century scribe who wrote the hortatory oracle which ended with these words:[3]

> But let justice roll down like waters,
> and righteousness like an everflowing stream (Amos 5:24).

An oracle with the same structure appears in the Deuteronomic introduction to the oracles of Isaiah (chapter 1). The oracle in Isaiah, which also de-emphasizes the practice of animal sacrifices and offerings, ends with a challenge:

> . . . cease to do evil, learn to do good;
> seek justice, rescue the oppressed,
> defend the orphan, plead for the widow (Isaiah 1:16–17).

The Deuteronomic Collection of Laws

The hortatory tone which characterized the two oracles referred to above (Amos 5:21–24 and Isaiah 1:12–17) permeates the torah of Deuteronomy (chapters 12–26). This exhortative quality has been referred to by scholars as *the law preached*.[4] Readers of the Deuteronomic torah are frequently encouraged to keep the law by the narrator or author. For example, after the law requiring the release of male and female slaves after six years of service, the following encouragement is given.

> Do not consider it a hardship when you send them out from you free persons, because for six years they have given you services worth the wages of hired laborers; and the LORD your God will bless you in all that you do (Deuteronomy 15:18).

This type of encouragement or exhortation does not appear in the other three collections of law in the Bible, the book of the covenant, the holiness code, or the priestly code.

The subject of the Deuteronomic torah, unlike the holiness code and the priestly code, is human relations, responsibility, cooperation, and interdependence. It becomes obvious, when the contents of the codes are compared, that two entirely different theological schools are involved. The Aaronid priests produced a code preoccupied with animal sacrifice, blood, cleanness, uncleanness, and concern for something called holiness. The book of Leviticus, representative of this non-Deuteronomic theology, is the product of the Aaronid priesthood.

The remaining law code in the scriptures is the so-called book of the covenant found in Exodus, chapters 21 to 23. It is obvious that the Deuteronomic torah is dependent to some extent on this ancient code. More than 50 percent of the laws in the book of the covenant appear in the Deuteronomic torah. There is a difference however. In the Deuteronomic code the laws are reworded and made more humane. The prime example of this is the law of the Hebrew slave. In Exodus it reads in part:

> When you buy a male Hebrew slave, he shall serve six years, but in the seventh he shall go out a free person, without debt. . . . If his master gives him a wife and she bears him sons and daughters, the wife and her children shall be her master's and he (the slave) shall go out alone (Exodus 21:2–6).

When the same law appears in Deuteronomy several significant changes are noted. (1) In the earlier law, found in the book of the covenant (BC), only a male debt-slave is set free. In Deuteronomy both a female and a male debt-slave are set free. (2) In BC the debt-slave receives freedom, but no provision. Deuteronomy states however:

> When you send the male slave out from you a free person, you shall not send him out empty-handed. Provide liberally out of your flock, your threshing floor, and your wine press, thus giving to him some of the bounty with which the LORD your God has blessed you. . . . You shall do the same with regard to your female slave (Deuteronomy 15:13–17).

(3) In BC the debt-slave must leave his wife and children behind if the master provided the wife. In Deuteronomy no mention is made of the master providing a wife. The family of the debt-slave is only his business. (4) In BC the employer is called a master six times. In Deuteronomy the word is not used. The word brother is used.

Here are five examples of the humanizing of law and the move in the direction of social justice found in the Deuteronomic version of BC (book of the covenant) laws:

(1) In BC a Hebrew father can sell his daughter as a slave (Exodus 21:7). There is no such law in Deuteronomy. In Deuteronomy a daughter can initiate a debt-slave agreement on her own however.

(2) In BC the law concerning the forced seduction of an unengaged virgin is concerned with the loss of the father's bride-price (*mohar*), not the plight of the young woman. In Deuteronomy (22:28) the virgin becomes a wife who cannot be divorced. The Deuteronomic version of the law is concerned with the protection of the violated woman, not the father's bride-price.

(3) In BC only the males make pilgrimages three times a year (Exodus 23:17). In Deuteronomy wives and daughters are included.

(4) In BC the oppression of a resident alien is forbidden (Exodus 23:9), but in Deuteronomy the Israelite is commanded to love the alien (10:19).

(5) In BC an animal that is not properly slaughtered is given to the dogs (Exodus 22:31). In Deuteronomy, where hunger is considered, the animal can be given to a non-Israelite.

We should also note that in Deuteronomy the reason for keeping the sabbath day is for humanitarian reasons. Every worker and every farm animal is entitled to a day of rest (5:15). In Exodus the reason given for keeping the sabbath is tied to the creation myth that God created the world in six days and rested on the seventh.

Ahab and Elijah

One of the most dramatic scenes in DH takes place when Elijah confronts Ahab in the vineyard of Naboth.[5] King Ahab says to Elijah:

Have you found me, O my enemy?

And Elijah replies:

Have you killed and also taken possession? (1 Kings 21: 17–20).

This dramatic scene followed the seizing of land belonging to Naboth following his execution as a result of the use of false witnesses hired by King Ahab and his wife Jezebel. Naboth had refused to give up his vineyard to the royal family because it was against the ancient code of rural Israel. Naboth said:

The LORD forbid that I should give you my ancestral inheritance (1 Kings 21:3).

The condemnation of the seizing of land by the powerful of Samaria and Jerusalem is a recurring theme in the scrolls preserved by the Deuteronomic circle. In Micah we read:

Alas for those who devise wickedness and evil deeds. . . .
They covet fields and they seize them;
houses and take them away;
they oppress householder and house,
people and their inheritance (Micah 2:1–2).

And the first of the seven woes of Isaiah, preserved for us by the Deuteronomic circle, refers to the ruthless land-grabber.

Ah, you who join house to house and field to field, until there is room for no one but you and you are left to live alone in the midst of the land (Isaiah 5:8).

Everywhere in DH the reader encounters justice themes. The ancient theme of Yahweh championing the poor and the weak appears in the song attributed to Hannah on the occasion of Samuel's birth.

The LORD makes the poor rich. . . . He raises up the poor from the dust; he lifts the needy from the ash heap to make them sit with princes (1 Samuel 2:7–8).[6]

In a song of Samuel we encounter the Deuteronomic theme of justice entwined with its de-emphasis on sacrifice and ritual:

Has the LORD as great delight in burnt offerings and
    sacrifices,
as in obeying the voice of the LORD?
Surely, to obey is better than sacrifice,
and to heed than the fat of rams (1 Samuel 15:22).

But it is in a Deuteronomic passage placed in Micah, which also entwines the Deuteronomic de-emphasis on animal sacrifice and offerings with the concern for social justice, that we encounter the most powerful summary statement of the Deuteronomic theology:

"With what shall I come before the LORD,
    and bow myself before God on high?
Shall I come before him with burnt offerings,
    with calves a year old?
Will the LORD be pleased with thousands of rams,
    with ten thousands of rivers of oil?
Shall I give my firstborn for my transgression,
    the fruit of my body for the sin of my soul?"
He has told you, O mortal, what is good;
    and what does the LORD require of you
but to do justice and love kindness,
    and walk humbly with your God? (Micah 6:6–8).

Summary

Pre-monarchical Israel was a loose federation of marginal groups living in the highlands and existing chiefly by subsistence farming. There was no powerful centralized political authority. On the contrary, there were many divisions in the land. El was the first God of Israel, but a group which scholars call *the Moses group*, which had a strong exodus tradition, introduced Yahweh as a more fitting God, one who would fight for the lower classes of society.

There were scattered shrines for the worship of both El and

Yahweh including Megiddo, Shechem, Shiloh, Bethel, Hebron, Beer-sheba, Gilgal, and others. There was no council on orthodoxy, no one person or group in charge of theology, and there was a diversity of local traditions. The unity of Israel which we read about in Deuteronomy and Joshua was an idealization of the past created by the passage of time, official scrolls of the united monarchy, and finally by the scribal activity of the Deuteronomic circle.

With the establishment of Jerusalem as a capital city for the house of David, the early chapter of Israel's history came to an end. Support for an ancient near eastern monarchy demanded a large supply of labor and resources to support the new upper classes of the urban area. Tremendous burdens were placed on the farmers of Israel.

The fact that Solomon's son, Rehoboam, had to go to Shechem to negotiate for his crown indicates that the Levitical priests of Shechem, like Yahweh their God, were recognized by the farmers of Israel as champions of the exploited classes of society. Rehoboam was rejected, and a northern monarchy was established with Jeroboam as the first king.

Jeroboam immediately recognized that the kind of monarchy he envisioned was inconsistent with the views of the Levitical priests and their deeply embedded perception of economic justice. Jeroboam moved his capital from Shechem to Penuel (and later to Tirzah). It is stated in DH that Jeroboam named Bethel and Dan as the two official state shrines, with Bethel chosen as competition for Jerusalem. We have noted that Bethel also became a competing shrine for Shechem. This is not stated in DH. In producing DH the scribes of the Deuteronomic circle during the reign of Josiah made a decision to keep a low profile for themselves and their ancestors, the Levitical priests of Shechem.

In the latter half of the 8th century at least two prophets delivered oracles in the name of Yahweh severely critical of the decision makers of Samaria, the capital city of Israel established by the house of Omri. These oracles of Hosea and Amos were preserved by the scribes of the Shechem priesthood and taken to Jerusalem after the tragic events of 722. The oracles of two southern 8th century prophets, Micah and Isaiah, were later added to the collection.

Until the days of Josiah, the Levitical priests of Shechem, both in Israel and later in Jerusalem, were outsiders, a fringe group in society. This location in society assisted them in preserving their ancient rural views of social justice. In no way were their scrolls preserved for the purpose of supporting or legitimizing the monarchy or the ruling class of society.[7]

The exact relationship between Josiah and the Deuteronomic circle is not clear for several reasons. (1) We don't know how large the group was or who its members were. (2) The account of Josiah's reign which we have is part pre-exilic and part exilic. It is part history, part folklore, and part theology.

What we do know is that Josiah was idealized by the scribes who produced DH, for theological and didactic purposes. Perhaps the most important fact about Josiah's reign, of which we can be certain, is that for the first time in 300 years Assyrian domination of Israel and the small nations of the western end of the fertile crescent was coming to an end as the Assyrian empire was terminally disintegrating. This was an opportunity for Judah to reunite the northern territories of Israel and restore the boundaries of David's ancient kingdom. The role which the Deuteronomists saw for themselves was the creation of a collection of scrolls embodying a theology based on the torah of Moses, a theology which enhanced both the majesty of God and the dignity of man.

With the sudden unexpected death of Josiah, Judah entered a period of rapid political decline, first as a vassal of Egypt, then as a vassal of neo-Babylon. Twenty-two years after the death of Josiah the city of Jerusalem and the temple were destroyed. The people of Yahweh became powerless people of exile. But they also became people of the book.

During the exile the Deuteronomists took DH and edited it, amended it, and enlarged it to speak to the new condition of Yahweh's people. They first had to explain why Yahweh had dealt so harshly with Judah. The answer emerged from the framework of a covenant relationship based on the vassal treaty form. This covenant relationship was envisioned as existing from the days of Moses. The people of Israel and Judah had continually violated the conditions of the covenant. Metaphors previously used to describe the relationship, parent-child, husband-wife,[8] were strengthened. In the introduction to the oracles of Isaiah these words were added:

> Hear, O heavens, and listen O earth;
> I reared children and brought them up,
> but they have rebelled against me (Isaiah 1:2).

Epilogue

When he has taken the throne of his kingdom he shall have
a copy of this law written for him in the presence of the
levitical priests (from the laws concerning the king in Deuteronomy 17:14–20).

We have commented in this chapter on the fact that the details
of the relationship between the Deuteronomic circle and King Josiah
are not accessible to us. We have made it clear, however, that in our
view the circle was not a rubber stamp for the monarchy and was not
under Josiah's control as a propaganda arm of the state. On the
contrary, our contention is that the Deuteronomic circle was completely independent and supported Josiah because of his compliance
with the Deuteronomic torah.

During the exile the Deuteronomists fulfilled their calling to
interpret the past by editing and expanding their scrolls. As a
closely knit circle, the Deuteronomists did not survive into the post-
exilic period. Their scriptures became the heart of the Hebrew Bible
and their influence can be seen in many post-exilic scrolls. Thousands of years later it can be said that there is not a Jew or a
Christian who has not been influenced by their powerful writings.

In the post-exilic period several additions were made to the
scriptures of the Deuteronomists.[9] The most significant passage appears in Joshua 24:1–28.

As a result of the work of the exilic editors, the metaphor of the
vassal-treaty form had permeated all the scriptures of the Deuteronomists, but a finishing touch was needed. For this purpose Joshua,
who had made his farewell speech in Joshua 23, was revived and
made young again. He gathered all Israel at Shechem (where else?)
and made a magnificent speech. (We remember that putting a
speech into the mouth of an ancient hero was a common practice in
ancient Israel.) This speech summarized the highlights of the first
Hebrew Bible. At its heart is this challenge:

. . . choose this day whom you will serve . . . but as for me
and my household, we will serve the LORD (Joshua 24:15).

NOTES

1. Recent scholars are examining the possibility that Amos
was a northern prophet rather than a Judean.

2. See the book by Robert Coote, *Amos Among the Prophets*, chapter 3, pages 46–109.

3. Ibid.

4. Gerhard von Rad, *Deuteronomy* (Philadelphia: Westminster, 1975), pages 19–20.

5. Our judgment identifies the confrontation between Elijah and Ahab as folklore, possibly based on a true incident, rather than history. Confrontation between kings and prophets are a recurring theme in DH. Our feeling is that these exchanges are folklore rather than history. The exchanges between Isaiah and Hezekiah are probably a mixture of history and folklore. In DH there is no report of the interchanges between Isaiah and Ahaz. These interchanges appear in the book of Isaiah (the memoirs) and are history.

6. The fact that the song ends with reference to a king does not mean that the original song comes from the period of the monarchy. The closing of the song could have been added by a scribe much later.

7. Several recent scholars have stated that the scriptures were produced by the ruling classes to promote their interests, but this book does not take that view. The Deuteronomic circle was not a rubber stamp for the monarchy. In Jeremiah we have an illustration of one monarch's view of Jeremiah's contribution to scripture. "As Jehudi read three or four columns, the king (Jehoiakim) would cut them off with a penknife and throw them into the fire in the brazier, until the whole scroll was consumed (read Jeremiah 36:20–32).

8. For an exilic expansion of the metaphor of the husband-wife relationship read Hosea 2:5–13.

9. For example, the account of the death of Moses in Deuteronomy 32:49–52 and 34:7–9 is attributed to the Priestly source (P). The paragraph in Deuteronomy 4:27–31, where the LORD is declared to be merciful ". . . who will not forget the covenant with your ancestors that he swore to them," is considered post-exilic. It is possible that Deuteronomy 1–3 was post-exilic to connect Deuteronomy and DH to the tetrateuch. Deuteronomy 4:41–43 and 30:1–10 are also considered post-exilic.

FOR FURTHER READING

Boadt, Lawrence. *Reading the Old Testament*. Mahwah: Paulist, 1984.

Coggins, Richard. *Introducing the Old Testament*. Oxford: New York, 1990.

Coogan, Michael David. "Joshua," *New Jerome Biblical Commentary*. Englewood Cliffs: Prentice-Hall, 1990.

Coote, Robert. *Early Israel*. Minneapolis: Augsburg-Fortress, 1990.

———, and Coote, Mary. *Power, Politics, and the Making of the Bible*. Minneapolis: Fortress, 1990.

———, and Ord, David, *The Bible's First History*. Philadelphia: Fortress, 1989.

Craigie, Peter. *Deuteronomy*. Grand Rapids: Eerdmans, 1979.

Cross, Frank Moore. *Canaanite Myth and Hebrew Epic*. Cambridge: Harvard, 1973.

Doorly, William J. *Prophet of Justice, Understanding the Book of Amos*. Mahwah: Paulist Press, 1989.

———. *Prophet of Love, Understanding the Book of Hosea*. Mahwah: Paulist, 1991.

Friedman, Richard Elliot. *The Exile and Biblical Narrative*. Chico: Scholars Press, 1981.

———. *Who Wrote the Bible?* New York: Harper and Row, 1987.

Garbini, Giovanni. *History and Ideology in Ancient Israel*. New York: Crossroad, 1988.

Gerbrandt, Gerald Eddie. *Kingship According to the Deuteronomistic History*. Ann Arbor: UMI, 1980.

Gottwald, Norman K. *The Hebrew Bible*. Philadelphia: Fortress, 1985.

———. *The Tribes of Yahweh*. Maryknoll: Orbis, 1979.

Gray, John. *I and II Kings*. Philadelphia: Westminster, 1975.

Hagstrom, David G. *The Coherence of the Book of Micah*. Atlanta: Scholars Press, 1988.

Hopkins, David. *The Highlands of Canaan*. Sheffield: JSOT, 1985.

King, Philip J. and Robert North. "Biblical Archaeology," *New Jerome Biblical Commentary*. Englewood Cliffs: Prentice-Hall, 1990.

Mayes, A.D.H. *Deuteronomy*. Grand Rapids: Eerdmans, 1991.

———. *Israel from Settlement to Exile*. Philadelphia: SCM Press, 1983.

Mays, James L. *Micah, A Commentary*. Philadelphia: Westminster, 1976.

McKenzie, Steven L. *The Chronicler's Use of the Deuteronomistic History*. Atlanta: Scholars Press, 1984.

———. *The Trouble with Kings*. Leiden: E. J. Brill, 1991.

Miller, Patrick, ed. *Ancient Israelite Religion*. Philadelphia: Fortress, 1987.

Mullen, E.T., Jr. *Narrative History and Ethnic Boundaries*. Atlanta: Scholars Press, 1993.

Nelson, Richard. *First and Second Kings*. Atlanta: John Knox, 1987.

———. *The Double Redaction of the Deuteronomistic History*. Sheffield: Scholars Press, 1981.

Nicholson, E.W. *Deuteronomy and Tradition*. Philadelphia: Fortress, 1967.

———. *God and His People*. Oxford: Clarendon, 1988.

Noth, Martin. *History of Pentateuchal Traditions*. Atlanta: Scholars Press, 1981.

Olyan, Saul M. *Asherah and the Cult of Yahweh in Israel*. Atlanta: Scholars Press, 1988.

Polzin, Robert. *Moses and the Deuteronomist*. New York: Seabury, 1988.

Rast, Walter E. *Joshua, Judges, Samuel, Kings*. Philadelphia: Fortress, 1978.

Stuhlmueller, Carroll. *New Paths Through the Old Testament*. Mahwah: Paulist, 1989.

Tey, Josephine. *The Daughter of Time*. New York: Macmillan, 1953.

Von Rad, Gerhard. *Deuteronomy*. Philadelphia: Westminister, 1975.

Weinfeld, Moshe. *Deuteronomy and the Deuteronomic School*. Oxford: University Press, 1983.

———. *Deuteronomy 1 to 11*. New York: Doubleday, 1991.

Wiseman, D.J. *The Vassal Treaties of Esharradon*. London, 1958.

Yee, Gale. *Composition and Tradition in the Book of Hosea*. New York: Scholars Press, 1987.

SUBJECT AND AUTHOR INDEX

164